A PEN
WAR DIARY

A frontline sketch book 1944-1945

Walter Hain

Introduced and edited by Peter Hain

*For Ad, wife, mother, grandmother, great
grandmother – and to many others, especially in
the anti-apartheid struggle, an inspiration too*

First Published 2015

Text and Illustrations
Copyright © Walter Hain 2015

Bretwalda Books
Unit 8, Fir Tree Close, Epsom,
Surrey KT17 3LD

info@BretwaldaBooks.com
www.BretwaldaBooks.com

ISBN 978-1-910440-34-6

Printed and bound in Great Britain by
Marston Book Services Ltd, Oxfordshire

Bretwalda Books Ltd

Contents

Acknowledgements

My thanks to my son Peter who worked on and edited the manuscript with me and pushed me to produce this booklet. His book, *Ad & Wal: values, duty, sacrifice in Apartheid South Africa* (Biteback, 2014), covers this wartime story as part of a much wider account of both my life and my wife's, especially in the freedom struggle against apartheid in the early 1960s when we lived in Pretoria.

I am very grateful to Matthew Ward for his Foreword and for so methodically scanning and arranging my wartime sketches and combining these with drafts from the diary I wrote when I served as a Signalman with C Company of the Royal Natal Carbineers, in Italy between 1944 until the Second World War ended in 1945.

I hope it captures the spirit of the time and stands as a record to the contribution to the War effort by my fellow soldiers, some of whom lost their lives in action.

My thanks to my wonderful wife Adelaine who has been the mainstay of my adult life ever since we were married in Pretoria in 1948, and who typed up the dairy from my original small handwritten one found in a captured house in Italy and which recorded what happened to me. This account is drawn from that diary in which I tried as meticulously as I could to log what I saw and experienced, whilst it was fresh in my mind.

I acknowledge with gratitude too my daughter-in-law Elizabeth Haywood for correcting the draft and the Commonwealth War Graves Commission for its kind permission to use its archive photographs from the South African Cemetery at Castiglione in the Apennines.

Amongst numerous books on the Italian campaign, I have drawn particularly upon two of the most authoritative to shed light on my experience: James Bourhill, *Come back to Portofino: Through Italy with the 6th South African Armoured Division* (Johannesburg, 30 Degree South Publishers, 2011), and Neil Orpen, *Victory in Italy* (Purnell, Cape Town, 1975).

I stress however that this booklet is a story based upon my original diary and sketches, rather than offering a fresh or deep analysis.

Walter Hain,
Vale of Neath, South Wales, September 2015

Introduction

L ike many ex-soldiers, my Dad always underplayed his role in the Second World War. 'I was very lucky not to be an infantryman fighting right on the frontline,' he always insisted.

But the action he describes in this book rather belies that modesty, and just occasionally his four children – Tom, Jo-anne, Sally and I – would be treated to a few recollections.

How a bullet from a German machine gunner, fired as he scampered through a vineyard below Monte Stanco, lodged in a can of corned beef in a shirt pocket over his heart, its force knocking him to the ground but mercifully not penetrating his chest. How one of his close comrades was killed right next to him in a trench, at the same time he was wounded.

His understated, underplayed role in the Second World War is actually belied by his own diaries which reveal a series of extremely narrow escapes, almost as if fate was on his side.

I always wondered about these and how I might so very easily never have existed.And how the same could be said of so many other sons and daughters – or would-be sons and daughters – of countless soldiers in battles over time immemorial.

We were also brought up – as were his many grandchildren, and even great-grandchildren – on a string of sometimes politically incorrect songs from his army days.

We loved them all, especially:

'Clink, clink, the glasses clink, making lovely music till the dawn is breaking.

'Bang, bang, who gives a damn, when we're out upon a spree?

'Over the teeth behind the gums, look out stomach here she comes.

'Have another drink with me – ee' ee.'

He was reluctant to acknowledge the legacy of his wartime experience and its influence upon him. But, just as in Britain after 1945 when demobbed soldiers determined on voting Labour whose landslide win ejected from office Churchill notwithstanding his famed wartime leadership, so, too, the Second World War had a radicalising impact on young, especially English-speaking, South African soldiers like my Dad.

His eyes were opened to the wider world of Europe and North Africa. Serving in the anti-Nazi cause, he became much more aware of its democratic values and of racial discrimination – in that case against Jews. Many young South Africans came to think seriously about their country's racial problems for the first time during World War 2.

Although my Dad, unassumingly as always, professed not to have had such an awakening, and did not easily reveal his inner emotions about the death and destruction he both witnessed and experienced, he was undoubtedly deeply affected in all sorts of ways.

One of the things which struck him forcibly was serving with South African black and Indian troops who were not permitted to bear arms – confined instead to stretcher-bearer and ancillary duties: 'servant' roles as they were back home in South Africa, defenceless yet right in the thick of extreme danger.

In the book I wrote about his life and that of my mother – *Ad & Wal: values, duty, sacrifice in Apartheid South Africa* (Biteback, 2014) – I tried to both understand and explain why this young white South African couple sacrificed almost everything for their belief in a non-racial society. For they – uniquely amongst their close relatives and friends – were amongst an infinitesimally small minority of whites whose commitment to fairness and justice for all led to great personal loss, and in their case exile for their young family.

He was also to become instinctively and sometimes implacably opposed to violence, telling me as a boy: 'Unless you have seen and experienced killing and carnage you cannot know how terrible it is, how people do such terrible things to each other.' He added; 'The problem with violence is it always breeds more violence.'

Yet he was never a pacifist. Thus, in 1963-4 when fiercely arguing with fellow white anti-apartheid activists engaged in sporadic acts of sabotage against state installations, his main case was that it would be counter-productive and invite even greater repression by the apartheid state – which indeed it did.

By contrast he supported Nelson Mandela's resort to underground guerrilla action when Mandela's African National Congress with its non-violent, constitutional tradition was made illegal under apartheid in 1960. My Dad argued that Mandela (citing the French Resistance adopting guerrilla tactics against the Nazis) had no alternative.

Like soldiers throughout time, he and his comrades, some killed, most surviving, were so very young, my Dad aged just eighteen at the start of his service. I think of myself and my two sons at that age, of many other youngsters I have met in peacetime, and wonder whether we would have all coped with the same stoic and understated commitment to duty? As in War, perhaps even more so in his subsequent role in the anti-apartheid struggle, his courage and modesty were notable.

Nobody is perfect, every one of us has flaws, but his life throughout has exhibited integrity, humility and dedication to the values he held dear: morality, justice, liberty, self-discipline, family and hard work. Old-fashioned values perhaps in this self-centred age, but invaluable, timeless ones surely?

To his children and grandchildren he had the characteristics of a 'Renaissance man'. He always knew what seemed to us to be a great deal about a wide range of subjects, from history to science, from art to literature, from politics to sport. He argued about philosophical questions with me, and about Black Holes with my elder son Sam, a physics student.

Although scrupulously courteous and polite, with a generous tolerance and a great sense of fun, he remained a man of firm convictions, often forcefully defending these with passion – for instance his implacable atheism which he explained to his children and grandchildren, always however respectful of those with religious beliefs.

As a father and family man, few could have been more devoted. Despite being in fulltime work as an architect in Pretoria, despite evenings and weekend hours spent on his anti-apartheid activism, he would always spare the time to help with homework, some of my essays in English lessons on current affairs raising quizzical eyebrows from my teacher: 'This writing bears a remarkable resemblance to the W. V. Hain who writes in the Rand *Daily Mail*!'

A couple of decades later, especially in retirement, he became similarly cherished by my two boys Sam and Jake, to whom he was a second father, and to his other grandchildren, going to watch them at their sport events, teaching them his old songs, talking to them, infectiously playing with them.

I remain immensely privileged to be the son of the best Dad in the world, this booklet granting only one, though important, insight into a very full life devoted almost entirely to others.

Peter Hain

Foreword

Apennine War Diary:

A frontline sketch book 1944-1945 is a fascinating collection of contemporaneous sketches (about 120 in total) and an accompanying diary, written by Walter Hain, aged 19 and 20 in 1944-45, when he served as a Signalman with C Company of the Royal Natal Carbineers during World War Two.

His diary – written in contravention of army rules during snatched moments of downtime – conveys the spirit of action, danger and death in combat. His distinctive neat writing, flowing prose and regular, conscientious entries revealed a characteristic orderliness, an organised mind.

Together with the sketches, it provides a unique insight into service on the front with the 8th Army fighting in Italy; an often neglected feature of the Allied resistance in Europe.

The sketches begin in Southern and then Northern Africa, but the main focus is on Walter's time fighting in the Apennine Mountains in Italy. Through his writing and drawing, Walter describes the daily routines and emotions of a soldier's life; the nervous anticipation and the sudden panic, the intimacy and friendship, but above all the surpassing sense of adventure. He also captures the colour and variety of the Apennine landscape; its beauty and serenity, a striking contrast with the ugly barbarity of war.

Walter's war reached a climax in 1944 at the battle of Monte Stanco. This crucial strategic position was held by the Germans until it fell into Allied control in October after a period of intense fighting. The most poignant and moving moment in the diary occurs later in the same month. His Afrikaner friend 'Lanky' Brasler – who features in his sketches – is mortally struck by a German shell as the pair are huddled in their shallow slit trench. Walter's attempts to save his friend are in vain. Wounded himself, then devastated at the loss of his comrade and companion, Walter was withdrawn from the frontline and after the War 1945 returned home to South Africa and his parents.

This was a foundational experience for the young man. It gave him a unique perspective on life which marked him out from many of his South

African contemporaries. Although Walter suffered injury and devastation at the loss of comrades, the diaries and sketches are remarkably sober and reflective. Throughout his later life – including, at great personal and family cost, his involvement in the anti-apartheid struggle in Pretoria – Walter's hatred for fascism and racism was never bellicose or frenzied. His wartime sketches reveal that humanity and compassion can endure even the most brutalising surroundings.

The South African 6th Armoured Division, in which he served, was established in 1943 during World War Two, the first of its kind in the South African army.

Whilst serving in Italy throughout 1944 and 1945, the Division was first attached to the British Eighth Army, but after the liberation of Florence, was transferred to the US Fifth Army. The commander throughout the war was Major General Evered Poole, a young and ambitious officer who eventually held senior diplomatic postings in the post-war apartheid government.

The Division was created to be the centrepiece of the South African contribution to the Allied war effort, organised by Prime Minister Jan Smuts, a hero of the First World War. The white South African political establishment had been torn apart over which side to support in the War, with many arguing for neutrality sympathetic to the Nazi regime.

The Division was trained in Egypt throughout 1943 and was originally destined to serve in Palestine. In the spring of 1943, however, there was a sudden change of plan and the Division departed for Taranto, Italy, making its way up the Italian peninsula at extraordinary speed.

After the liberation of Rome, the north of Italy remained fiercely contested and the Division was at the forefront of the Allied advance. From Rome the Division marched east along the Tiber; the liberation of Florence its key strategic objective. After heavy fighting, members of the Kimberley Regiment entered Florence across the Ponte Vecchio in July 1944, the first Allies coming into the city.

The Allies wasted no time in thrusting further north into the Apennine Mountains; aiming to attack and dissolve the Germans' last defensive position in northern Italy, the so-called 'Gothic Line'. Having secured this position by February 1945, the Division was involved in the 'Spring Offensive' into the Lombardy Plain in the far north of the country. Their forces wounded and heavily depleted, the Germans staged one last attempt to resist Allied control of Italy. There was vicious fighting throughout the operation and the Division suffered heavy casualties. About 900 members of the Division were killed or died in Italy, with about 1800 South Africans in total buried in the war cemeteries in Italy.Eventually, however, the key cities of Bologna and Milan were taken by the Allies; the final, fatal blow to fascist Italy, Hitler's ally.

With the war over, the Division returned to South Africa and was disbanded in 1946. It was briefly reinstated from 1 July 1948 to 1 November 1949, but never again saw such intense action as it had in the mountains of central and northern Italy.

What follows is Walter's own account, based on his diary, including his sketched map of his route through the Apennine region. The first set of sketches was produced in Africa, whilst Walter's unit was preparing for war in Europe, the following two sets of sketches from Italy in 1944 and 1945.

There are then three appendices. The first of these is an outline of his war itinerary. The second is a typed copy of the full diary, fifteen pages in total, and the third is a selection of pages from the original small pocket diary in which he wrote.

The structure is intended to be simple and accessible, allowing Walter's striking artistic insight and skill to come to the fore and for the content to speak for itself.

Matthew Ward

Prologue

It was morning on 21 October 1944 when I was aged nineteen, my fellow army radio operator 'Lanky' Brasler[1] aged eighteen.

We had moved to Point 806 high on Monte Pezza, a mountain in the Apennines, and among some trees we stumbled across a 'slittie' (slit trench) wide enough to take both of us.

We were both surprised and delighted, because in months of action it was the only one like that we'd ever discovered. Normally a slittie was a one-man trench, long and deep enough to protect a soldier from shell shrapnel and flying bullets. More often than not we had been forced to toil away in the hard, unyielding soil to dig out a suitable slittie. Although we were young and fit, it was backbreaking.

So we delightedly occupied this one, and immediately tried to make it more secure from overhead shell bursts. We gave it a roof of tree branches topped with a layer of soil, and a gap at one end for access. In my daily diary I recorded that we 'felt as safe as a house', because we couldn't believe out luck.

Lanky and I were young Privates in the 6th South African Armoured Division, part of the British 8th Army which, with the American 5th Army, was driving the German forces occupying Italy northwards out of the country. Our infantry battalion was the Royal Natal Carbineers (RNC), and we were in C Company.

That morning our Company took over a frontline position from B Company, which is why we were able to move straight into their existing slitties. I was constantly apprehensive during the War and sometimes downright terrified. But even when, around ten o'clock, German shells started coming over a hill to our left, we both still felt very safe and were trying to sleep.

That all changed two hours later, when shells began bursting nearby with shrapnel flying everywhere. The din was terrifying, not least because shrapnel seemed to have a knack of going in all directions, sometimes it seemed even around corners.

We were suddenly trapped in our 'safe as houses trench', the Germans pounding our lines. There seemed no escape. Then – shockingly – our worst fear: shrapnel tore straight through the access opening in the trench

---

[1] Private G. C. Brasler, son of Mr and Mrs A.B.M. Brasler of Clanwilliam, Cape Province, South Africa

roof near our feet. It should not have been able to do so: it seemed to come from the rear rather than the direction of fire.

I felt a sudden stabbing impact in the top of my right thigh, in the groin, and quickly put my hand down to make sure the family jewels were intact – to my utter relief they were.

But Lanky shouted: 'I've been hit, I've been hit.' 'So have I,' I shouted back. In response – and to my horror – Lanky jumped straight out the opening of the slittie and began calling for help. But then another shell arrived and Lanky grabbed his back and began screaming 'Oh Mama, Mama, Mama.'

It was sheer pandemonium. As I desperately pulled Lanky back down into the slittie and tried to prop him up, he moaned heartrendingly. In the confusion and the clash of my emotions it was obvious Lanky was badly hurt – very badly.

Fortunately our Company medical orderly 'Dutch' soon arrived and gave Lanky morphine. I willed it to make him better, but it seemed not to do so. I tried to offer reassurance by repeatedly telling him 'You will be alright.' But despite my increasingly desperate expressions of comfort and optimism, Lanky seemed sure he wasn't going to make it. 'No, no,' he kept groaning, and then said: 'Promise to go and see my sister. Tell her what happened.'

'No, you will be alright,' I urged him. 'Just hang on. Stretcher-bearers will soon be coming to take to you safety.'

And, indeed, ignoring incoming fire, South African Indian stretcher-bearers soon rushed in. They reached down to carry Lanky away to the regimental aid post nearby, in a large house called Casa Ruzzone.

I just assumed he would be okay as I looked hurriedly around to grab what I could of our things, and dragged myself awkwardly out of the slittie, not knowing whether I too would be mortally hit by shrapnel still raining down everywhere.

Pain was now shooting from my thigh as I limped towards Casa Ruzzone myself. My mind was swirling, I guess with shock as a little way up a path I bumped into the stretcher-bearers having a breather. 'How is Lanky,' I asked expecting the best.

'Dead,' they replied, not insensitively but matter-of-fact.

Surely not? I was stunned, couldn't believe it.

Almost immediately I was consumed with a dreadful sense of guilt that it was when Lanky had jumped out, calling for help for both of us –

maybe more so for me – that the second shell had killed him.

I had been through some scrapes earlier since arriving in Italy. I had witnessed other comrades killed and injured, and I counted myself lucky that I was a signalman coming in behind the frontline fighters who took most casualties. I had enlisted enthusiastically in the war effort. But now I felt overcome by a dulling, deadening despair.

Forty-one years later, in 1985, I retraced my steps from Monte Cassino through Rome into the Apennines aided by my old wartime diary, accompanied by Adelaine, Peter, his wife and two small boys. It was both exhilarating and discomforting going back because it was so very different as to be hardly recognisable. I never much liked talking about what I had experienced, though I had told the family some of the main events.

A week or so into the trip Peter drove us around a corner in his old Volkswagen Camper Van, coming into the tiny village of Castiglione dei Pepoli which was in my diary.

There, quite unexpectedly, we saw a sign for a Commonwealth War Graves Commission Cemetery for South African soldiers, set in a beautiful vale, a kaleidoscope of green shades with a sprinkling of brightly coloured flowers, birds tweeting in the sunshine: utter peace and tranquillity. So different from the last time I had driven through Castiglione. (The village now even has a street named after the 6th South African Armoured Division.)

I was both curious and eager, yet also uncertain. My fallen comrades might be buried there, yet I hadn't even known it existed. The family encouraged me to stop. Yes I should do so – though at the same time I was dreading it, for by now we were into the region where the War had been worst for me.

It turned out to contain 502 burials by the 6th South African Armoured Division in which I served, and which entered Castiglione in September 1944, many of these direct from Apennine battlefields north of the village until April 1945.

To the left, down a little from the entrance we saw a small stone building. Entering we found a metal-encased ledger, and in it – yes – Lanky's name recorded alongside the location of his grave.

I was both elated but also filled with deep melancholy. My emotions swirled as I walked down a slope, and through rows and rows of white-

13

grey headstones, stark, sombre and yet dignified in the serene sunshine.

Eventually, passing graves bearing names of others I had known, there was Lanky's.

Such another realm, such a lifetime ago. I almost wasn't sure what to do, what to feel – being someone who tended to bottle up rather than to show emotion.My family noticed afterwards that my eyes were moist; certainly there was a large lump in my throat.

I knelt down on one my knee both out of respect and to photograph his headstone – conscious of an inescapable image of fate: had our positions in that slittie been reversed, it could well have been Lanky and his family visiting my own gravestone in that beautiful setting.

The South African Cemetery at Castigleoni, which is maintained by the Commonwealth War Graves Commission. The cemetery contains 502 Commonwealth burials of the Second World War. The majority of those buried in this cemetery were South Africans, the remainder belonging mostly to the 24th Guards Brigade, which was under command of the 6th South African Armoured Division.

CHAPTER 1

Volunteer

I was just fourteen and still at school when Germany invaded Poland in 1939 triggering the outbreak of the Second World War, having been born in Northdene, a suburb of Durban, a South African from a country at the southern tip of the continent run by two white, sometimes antagonistic groups.

Mine was English-speaking, the other Afrikaans – a language which evolved from a variety of Dutch, Flemish and French Huguenot settlers. When war broke out in 1939 all English-speaking whites   even boys like me – wanted to become involved on the British side, though only a few Afrikaners who had a deep, historic grievance against Britain. (And with considerable justification: concentration camps were a British invention during the Boer Wars at the end of the nineteenth century and 25,000 Afrikaner women and children died in them.)

My father Walter and two older brothers Bill and Tom quickly enlisted, as did any others of suitable age, and were involved in the military campaign to drive Hitler's allies, the Italians, from Abyssinia (Ethiopia) in 1940–41. They then returned back home. Meanwhile, I had moved with my mother Mary from where we were then staying in Johannesburg, back to Pretoria and I enrolled at Pretoria Boys High School where Bill had once been captain of cricket.

English-speaking teenage boys like me were keen as mustard to join up. It just seemed the natural thing to do. I knew war was dangerous but nevertheless felt driven like all my friends to volunteer.

I was hardly aware at the time that, unlike in Britain, there was no conscription. The South African Parliament had decided only narrowly (by just thirteen votes) to support the Allies rather than the Nazis.

The Second World War had divided South Africa's white population, British descendants like us backing the Allies, Afrikaners siding heavily with the Nazis. Some of their leaders, including a future Prime Minister, John Vorster, were interned for pro-Nazi activity including sabotage of Allied troop trains.

Ben Schoeman, an Afrikaner and later a Cabinet minister for twenty-six years, had said in 1940: 'The whole future of Afrikanerdom is dependent on a German victory.' I remember the tale of a German U-boat submarine abortively landing a former Afrikaner South African boxing champion on the west coast, having trained him in sabotage – he was arrested and jailed.

But – much to my frustration – my Dad insisted I continue with my studies. Despite my pleas, he wouldn't allow me to enlist until I turned eighteen at the end of 1942.

I matriculated with a First Class Secondary School Certificate at the end of 1941, including a Distinction in art which I found I was good at, having sketched from an early age. Dad, struck by my artistic ability, had already encouraged me to train as an architect and I went from school to work as an architectural assistant for Pretoria municipality during the day, studying in the evening for the five-year degree in architecture for which I had been accepted at Johannesburg's Witwatersrand University.

A year later, now aged eighteen and despite enjoying my work and studying, I was still determined to serve in the war. I had always dreamt of becoming a fighter pilot, and went early in 1943 to Waterkloof military airfield outside Pretoria to apply.

The normal tests began encouragingly well. Then, abruptly, my dream was shattered. A test found me unable to distinguish some colours – apparently a form of colour blindness – which barred me from being a pilot. It was a savage blow – made worse since it was so unexpected. I had never been aware of this impairment before.

Bafflingly, my art teacher considered me an excellent artist and nobody else had ever noticed this disability either. Utterly bereft, I didn't wait for a bus and instead walked ten miserable miles home. I felt as if my whole world had collapsed.

However my Dad, who was now a captain in the Engineers stationed at Sonderwater, east of Pretoria, said there was a shortage of signallers and suggested I should join the Signal Corps.

I wasn't that keen frankly, but decided anyway to go to the recruiting office. There I was pleased to meet up with an old school friend, Brian Blignaut, who had also decided to become a signaller. Brian was six feet four inches tall and I ended up referring to him as 'Loftus', later to become his army nickname.

Eventually – and much to my relief – I was accepted into the army aged eighteen at the beginning of 1943. I received basic training at the town of Potchefstroom and then at various locations in Natal, with my friends Loftus and Pete de Klerk.

Months of training seemed to consist of lots of square bashing coupled with the much more interesting radio electronics.

Finally we got serious, boarding at Durban docks on a troop ship, the converted French luxury liner Ile de France, on 30 April 1943, arriving in Egypt at Suez a fortnight later.

Serious overcrowding on board meant that, once the ship started rolling in heavy seas, the rail was lined with men throwing up over the side. Serried ranks also about to throw up stood a few paces behind; as soon as convulsions seized one of the latter he would shout a warning, and someone bending over the rail would step aside as he flung himself forward to puke. I took my turn with the rest. It wasn't a pretty sight.

Loftus at the signals Training Unit in Durban, while waiting to embark on the ship for training in Egypt

On the ship 'Ile de France', travelling from Durban up to Egypt

CHAPTER 2

Egypt

As we neared the port of Suez I was eager to see what awaited, for Egypt brought back school lessons on Pharaohs, mummies and pyramids, but I had never imagined actually being there. We landed at a quay, carrying our kit down gangways in a great mass, my closest signaller friends Loftus and Pete de Klerk like me looking around at the strange surroundings.

There were palm trees and Arab men in robes, women mostly in headscarves.

We headed over to board an overnight troop train for Cairo. But soon our animated buzz was replaced with intense, annoying irritation. The carriages, packed to bursting with our soldiers, were infested with bugs which seemed to find every nook and cranny of our bodies.

The itchiness seemed endless and got in the way of trying to sleep. Yet that was all forgotten as we passed the pyramids towering outside the city, an awesome size and presence. Still aged only eighteen, our mission seemed like a great, exhilarating adventure.

Our train journey continued south along the river Nile to Khatatba in the dry scorching desert outside Helwan, where we disembarked. Here I was to be trained as a radio operator in the 14th South African Signals Brigade. After completing our training we were posted to the Royal Natal Carbineers (RNC), in C Company.

Most of our time was spent learning how to use our radio equipment, and how to carry and deploy it effectively in combat. We were also instructed how to lay communication lines.

Army life, especially in a North African Arab country, was an eye-opener for me, innocent in many ways and I suppose by many standards perhaps unworldly. Mine was very much a boy's upbringing – girls were almost a foreign species, to be respected but not touched. I also felt different because, unlike my colleagues, I was teetotal and did not smoke.

Being stationed outside Cairo we were allowed to visit quite often on leave breaks and I jumped at the chance every time. Its ancient wonders were captivating, especially the Pyramids which were even more massive when you got right up to them.

My friends and I were intrigued by what we were told was a soldiers' frequent haunt, the local brothel, 'Sister Street'. We hadn't been inside a brothel before and decided to investigate why it had a reputation for being notorious. Discovering a walkway in front of a line of prostitutes' rooms, with women sitting outside dressed only in panties, we watched as customers circulated to make their choices and be taken inside.

I certainly was having none of that, but as we walked closely by, one of the women reached out and to my horror snatched off my army cap. She quickly turned to take it inside but, much to my relief I was able to grab it back immediately and make a hasty retreat – a narrow escape!

Another encounter with women was much more comfortable. After several years apart it was nice to have the chance to meet up again with my older brothers Bill and Tom who were in a different regiment but also stationed at Khataba, having previously been fighting the Italians in Abyssinia (now Ethiopia).

Bill and Tom had been to Alexandria for a weekend break where they had met some British army girls and taken them to the beach for a swim. They gave the girls' names to me and with Loftus and Pete met up in the same way, really enjoying what I suppose by 21st century standards might be viewed as a boringly platonic outing. It was great fun chatting and swimming with them all, though being quite shy I left most of the talking to my friends, and at the end of the afternoon they went back to their quarters.

My friends and I stayed in a coastal resort where the strangest thing we encountered was a mystery fitting in the bathrooms of our small hotel; none of us had the faintest idea what a bidet was for.

Programme of Anniversary celebrations, after arriving in Khatabah 1942-1943

For Your
Entertainment

"DECIBELLES"   ORCHESTRA
Trumpet, Sig Taylor.   Drums, Cpl Rorke.
Violin, Sig Eade.   Guitar, Sig O'Ehley.

GUEST ARTIST—L/BDR REG CLAYTON.

PROGRAMME.

Overture   Orchestra.
Song — Selected   Cpl. Rorke.
The Hill-Billy Boys   Sigs. Pool & Morgan.
Cornet Solo   Cpl. Hyde.
Humorous Sketch   Sig. Betts.
Song — Selected   Sig. Pool.
Violin Solo   Sig. Houseman.
            Reg Clayton & his Accordion.
Song — Selected   Cpl. Rorke.

Signal training vans in use in Helwan near Khatatba, July 1943

Bungalow at
the training
grounds in
Helwan

EGYPT 1943

Signallers training in 1943 in Egypt, Loftus seated
with myself behind him

Loftus training in a wireless van at Khatatba

Loftus and Pete de Klerk training in Khatatba on the 18 radio set

24

Knocked-out German
tank at Khatatba

Sketch at Khatatba of
Germans, a German
tank and a South
African tribal boy

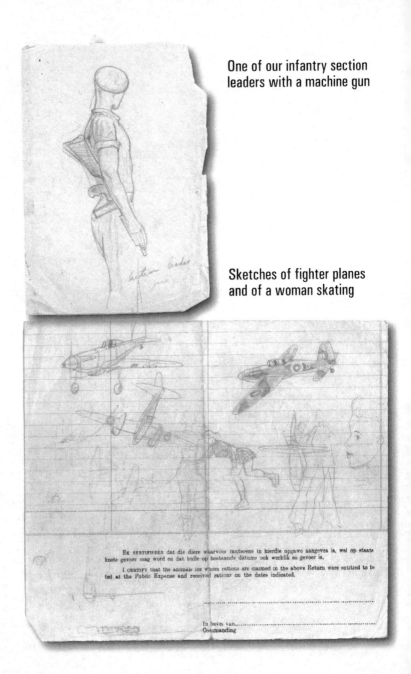

One of our infantry section
leaders with a machine gun

Sketches of fighter planes
and of a woman skating

Pete de Klerk reading at Khatatba

Rifles, uniform and sundry items stacked up around a tent pole at Khatatba

Loftus writing home inside a tent at Khatatba

A training radio vehicle at Khatatba, with two soldiers taking a nap in its shade

In the Desert outside Cairo

Anti-tank guns training in the desert near Helwan outside Cairo

Blignaut (Loftus) writing home while training at Khatatba

Sketches of Egyptians at Khatatba

Sherman Tank while we trained at Khatatba

MESSAGE FORM

Sherman Tank at Khatatba

Troops resting in Khatatba, yachts in the Nile River and
an Egyptian with a horse drawn cart

CHAPTER 3

Action Starts in Italy

Our training and preparation had lasted for nearly a year before we were deemed ready for combat action. It had been almost a limbo existence and we were chafing at the bit.

The prospect was exciting: this was what I had come for. None of us were worried. Although we all felt uncertain about what lay ahead, and knew it would now get serious, there was more of a spirit of a next stage in our great adventure than any sense of foreboding.

My unit left Port Said on 12 April 1944 aboard the ship *Ascania*, and this time the journey across the Mediterranean was far smoother than our previous one. Nine days later, on 21 April, we landed at Taranto on the southern tip of Italy, all of us excited and intrigued yet also nervous as we disembarked to this new land.

It was warm spring weather, as we began our slow convoy to the town of Gravina, about 60 miles away.It was an opportunity simply to take in our new surroundings because there was no threat down in this part of the country, the Allies having already pushed the Germans about 200 miles further up North East beyond Gravina where we stayed for a week. We then pushed on, with Naples to our West, stopping over south east of the town of Cassino on 1 May, only too aware from our commanders of the raging battle which we were about to join.

The Allied advance had been halted there for four months of carnage and our battalion moved into a holding position, relieving a Canadian division just outside the town on 4 May. Towering above us, it was obvious how the Germans had been able to resist Allied forces by controlling the summit of Cassino Mountain. It commanded the town at its foot and provided both formidable attack positions and observation of the country for some ten miles around.

A famous Benedictine monastery dating back to A.D. 529, the Abbey of Monte Cassino crowned the peak like a sheer rock outcrop. German forces were entrenched all the way up the steep mountain sides and in the town itself, mercilessly pounding all our Allied forces. Whatever you tried to do, the Monastery's eyes seemed to look right at you.

On 11 May our final assault on Cassino began in earnest. Now aged nineteen, I joined my unit in the Allied line on 15 May. On the night before, the foremost infantry units filtered silently back to a safety line and from 8.30 on the morning of the 15 May, Allied bombing of the town, mountain and monastery began – by noon, when it ceased, some 500 aircraft had dropped more than 1,000 tons of bombs. Only then did the Allies begin advancing into the town and up the mountain, in the face of still very determined resistance from enemy machine gunners and snipers. I could see blood everywhere until rain after dusk washed some of it away. All hell had broken loose.

Although still high on adrenalin, and based in a holding position back from the front, I was astounded by the scale of the action to the fore. Planes roared continuously overhead. There was a deafening thumping of bombs and billowing smoke. I was both exhilarated by my first experience of action, and yet living on my nerves. The dulling anti-climax was the proverbial predicament of the army private – lots of hanging around and very little information.

Long, long hours dragged by, and I used this to write up the diary which I had tried to update regularly. I knew it was forbidden under army regulations to keep a diary because it was a potential source of intelligence if captured.But I had always had something of a rebellious streak lurking underneath the instinctively polite and respectful manners drilled into me by my upbringing. The diary was quite detailed, my handwriting regarded as very clear and neat, often in pencil (which I always kept on me).

'I went up and joined our troops in the line. We were in prepared positions which Allied troops had occupied for months, there was a lot of rubbish and debris around, no showers or latrines and the place smelled.' I was on the reverse slope of a hill and incoming German shells 'ripped over us'.

After what seemed an interminable time – for there seemed no end in sight – by 18 May both Cassino town and mountain had finally been taken. The fine medieval monastery was destroyed, and the successful Allied advance towards Rome began.

But this achievement had been at an appalling cost to the Allies. In this battle for Cassino about 200,000 Allied men – including British, Americans, New Zealanders, French, Poles, Indians and Gurkhas – were either killed or wounded. (German fatalities were around 25,000.) It was certainly the most brutal single conflict in the entire war.

On the one hand I was thrilled we had won this vital battle. On the other I was appalled at the monumental scale of death and destruction: it was almost impossible to comprehend.

Wounded German prisoner being taken into captivity on Monte Pezza. The feet in the background are of a German machine gunner, killed in our attack

My original sketch of the Monte Pezza wounded German ('Ted')*, made when I had no ink
*The Italian for German being Tedesco or Tedeschi in plural

Sketched after the war, looking from Pezza towards Stanco at sunset

PANZANO.

Loftus, Lanky and I in our own slitties next to officer's
jeep at Panzano during the advance to Florence

Lanky Brasler, 'Lang en Maer' (Afrikaans for long and thin)

C Company Dutch medical orderly treating a wounded comrade in a house

An imagined comrade who has been killed by an
88 high explosive German shell landing near him

**Signaller Johnnie working a night shift
at Fornelli 12 May, 1944**

A week after the carnage had
thankfully ended at Cassino, I was
withdrawn to Fornelli and I 'had porridge
with milk for the first time for a week',
immensely relieved I had not been
advanced enough for the four months of
slaughter which finally pushed the
Germans off Monte Cassino and out of
the town.

I had now been allocated to the RNC
Support Company's Bren gun carrier
platoon. The lightly armoured carriers,
used mainly for reconnaissance, were
small, roofless, tracked vehicles, with the

driver and a Bren gunner in the front and one seat on each side of the engine in the back. As a radio operator, I travelled with a Number 22 set in the back of the platoon commander's carrier (when the platoon commander was in a carrier, he would act as the Bren gunner).

We drove carefully, picking our way along roadsides which had been strewn with mines by our retreating enemy. But what shocked me most was the sight of the towns we entered: it was hard to see how people were somehow clinging on to life amidst the chaotic debris. On 31 May we arrived north of Pontecorvo to find it so battered as scarcely habitable. Road sides here strewn with Teller [anti-tank mines] and box [anti-personnel mines].'

On 3 June 1944, 'Our boys giving it stick at Paliano', we parked next to an artillery battery and incoming German shells blew up one of their parked carriers; fortunately it was empty.

But the next day we were all elated to hear the news that the Americans had taken Rome; it was a symbol of our onward progress and success in driving the Germans back. A couple of days later, on 6 June we learnt even better news as it trickled through: it was the 'D Day' of the Allied Normandy beach landings, and we waited anxiously to hear the outcome, but news was hard to come by.

Our 'D Day' was 'R Day' as our carrier moved through Rome. My school history lessons came alive as there were so many breath-taking glimpses, not that we had a moment for sight-seeing as we drove amidst the 'populace lining roads and cheering, a very clean, fine city with very good-looking women'. Rome, I had learnt, was known as the 'Open City' because its irreplaceable historic heritage encouraged an agreement between the Allies and Germans not to fight in it.

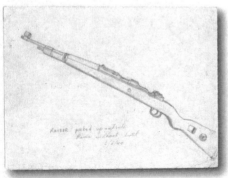

German Mauser without bolt, rifle picked up outside Rome on 6 June, 1944

38

CHAPTER 4

North of Rome

From Rome we moved thirty miles north on the Via Flaminia to Civita Castellana, the first of series of walled towns on hills, surrounded by lush ravines. For centuries one day's ride from Rome, it had been a place to stop and change horses, but there was no opportunity to savour the pretty area around with its tufa cliffs, gorges and Etruscan burial sites. Instead I noted that the main road through consisted of old, rendered, colour-washed buildings with curved tiles on the roofs, balconies and flower boxes everywhere.

Then we came upon Viterbo, its medieval centre preserved within a stone wall, sitting astride a hill with long views of the plains and lakes around.

There was no engagement yet with the Germans retreating towards Florence. But on the twisty road down from Montefiascone, another typical hilltop town, was Lake Bolsena. It was ringed by hills, with a cacophony of croaking frogs and 'knocked out Panther and Tiger tanks that lined the road on the west side of the lake'.

Continuing north through sunken, leafy lanes, we were now on the tail of the Germans, in a 'Bren gun carrier probing gingerly forward to make contact with the enemy'. In the rolling country near Belvedere, we stopped up some little tracks to replenish energy in a splendid captured farmhouse which I sketched.

Afterwards we drove past the position where 'a Spandau scythed down seven comrades from D Company' who had taken some prisoners in the engagement. It was eerie sleeping nearby and I recorded an incident that seemed to summarise the casual brutality of War, even comrade-to-comrade: 'Dead Jerry aged 18 lying in the trees. Two German prisoners buried him. Grave too short so they jumped on his ankles until these broke then stuffed his feet in. His cross said "Died for Greater Germany".'

The weather was warm and fair throughout this period of my action in Italy over the summer and into the autumn.But despite my keen eye for the greens of all shades in the sweep of hills and the kaleidoscope of colour – red poppies in field after field, bright flowers and bushes – the

39

tempo of action left me little time to enjoy the beautiful countryside. Stunning Tuscany largely passed me by, the breath-taking Apennines with their little villages tucked away hardly registered. It was as if we were in a war cocoon, traversing a land which, really only when I visited again forty years later, did I truly comprehend was breath-taking.

German 88 Anti-tank gun at Viterbo

88 at Viterbo

Imagined sketch done near Greve of Loftus in a slittie behind all the signalling equipment used in a position

near greve

Above, drawing of houses on hilltop in last yellow rays of sun about 10 miles south of Belvedere on 16 June 1944. Below, a grey cloudy day drawing of a house D Company took near Belvedere on 18 June, 1944, losing five fellows in the process.

On 22 June 1944 'Watched M-10s (self-propelled guns) giving a house hell. Saw Loftus in a house on a hillside and got some magazines. Wonderful site but Huns have ruined pictures, furniture & library. Shelled a bit.'

Later, through twenty miles of twisting roads, there was fighting all around us: one 'lot got mucked up', and I 'watched Jerries shelling a road and saw a despatch rider go for a loop' (crash and die). I was very nervous but pent up as we passed the hill-top town of Cetona; and I 'sketched from atop the carrier' its distinctive town tower.

In these comfortable little Umbrian towns life had been flowing gently by – as it had done for generations and would do again after the War – but now on 26 June in Chiusi there were 'shattered houses with outside walls blown away, bedding hanging out forlornly and personal possessions strewn obscenely around'.

There was more fighting: 'Roy and Mac wounded.' But then I found an opportunity in the little town: 'Got some good books. (Also the diary in which am writing).' Two days later having left Chiusi, A Company 'had good show, killed 8 and took 11 prisoners, lost 2 killed'.

Despite the ferocity and killing around me, the few family members who decades later read these diary entries observed that they were largely factual, sometimes capturing the heady excitement and danger, rarely revealing my emotions. But I would have felt uncomfortable doing so: traditionally brought-up boys like me kept our feelings bottled up inside, we didn't parade them around in front of others. I was simply recording what happened to me.

The Tower at Cetona, sketched on the morning of the 22 June 1944

Pushing forward in pursuit of fleeing German forces, I called by regional headquarters, and was thrilled to see my elder brothers Tom and Bill who were signallers with an artillery unit.

Then on 3 July I was transferred from the Bren gun carriers to C Company signals team with my new signals partner, Letsie. However, that partnership was sadly all too brief, because only a few days later, on 9 July, Letsie 'copped it'.

Although I've never been a spiritual man, in retrospect I suppose fate must have been on my side as it was to remain throughout the weeks ahead. On 9 July 'Letsie copped it today.' He and I went to have a bath at the well in a little village, Rapale. 'Letsie washed. When he'd finished I took the bath round the corner to fill it at the well. As I was pumping the first shell landed – didn't hear the explosion as much as shrapnel whistling everywhere. I think it was this one that got Akker (Letsie – we called him Akker because he'd been circumcised so had an akkerpiel – acornprick). I dived next to the wall, RDLI blokes too. About 3 more arrived right on top of us. I dived next to the wall. Masonry tumbled down just behind me. When all quiet I shot round the corner to find Letsie being attended to by a medical orderly – a shell had sliced off one leg above the shin and he was in a lot of pain. They had radioed for the MO and ambulance jeep. I went back to see what was going on and there were two men unconscious in the rubble. The RDLI blokes were there and it was decided not to move them – heard later they had died. I collected Letsie's clothes and took them to our possie near the road and when the ambulance jeep came past with him handed the clothes to them. Loftus came up to replace Lets in our team. So we are together again at last. Slept in the rain. Jerry shelled us at about 2 in the morning.'

In action, my company consisted of three platoons (8, 9 and 10) – the soldiers who actually did the fighting – and a headquarters section (HQ). This had a commander (a major), an intelligence officer (Stan Jones) who carried the maps and orders for attacks and a two-man signals team, myself and Loftus (who had now taken Letsie's place), to keep the major in touch both with battalion HQ and with his platoons through Lanky. In normal action the HQ section was out of sight of the enemy and did not receive small arms fire, though it did receive shell and mortar fire. The signals team radio came in two sections which had to be connected up, together with a heavy car-sized battery, headphones, microphone and tubular steel aerials. When it was being taken into action, Loftus carried the larger section on his back and I the smaller one, with the battery, other bits and his rifle in his hands. When not being carried this radio set was in the major's Jeep as were Loftus and I. Lanky's set was a one-piece, smaller and carried on his back.

Signal-man fixing a break

Fixing a break

Signalmen laying radio wires

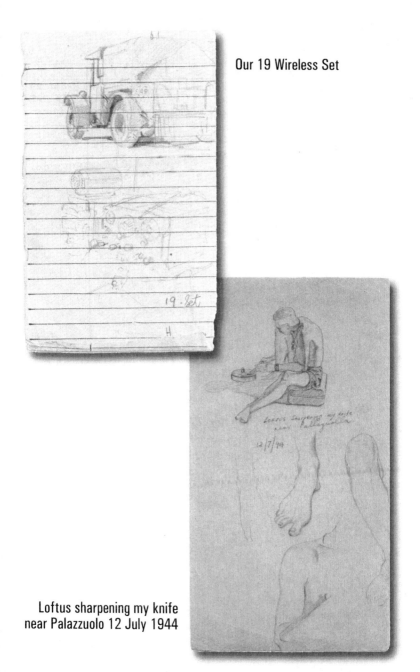

Our 19 Wireless Set

Loftus sharpening my knife
near Palazzuolo 12 July 1944

45

Myself using a mirror and having breakfast near Palazzuola 14 July, 1944

On the job, using wiring equipment; self-portrait, near Palazzuola on 18 July 1944

In the days that followed the loss of Letsie, I travelled in the major's Jeep with my radio, my diary repeatedly recording 'deadly', with colleagues killed or wounded.

We were still pushing the Germans back, but they were resisting all the way.Most of the time I wasn't sure what was really happening. I simply carried on, doing my duty. But death and menace lurked around every corner, up every rise, down every vale.

At Panzano, we sheltered in slitties we had had dug right next to our Jeep: 'Tanks above road. Bazooka & Spandau on corner. Shelling quite close. Spent chunk hit my book about 6 inches from Lanky's face, another ricocheted off left front wheel past my face into ground beside Lanky.'

There was more fighting and horror to come as the hot days in late July flew by. 'Smith hit, Corbett and McMorran badly ... Next day [26th] quiet – Sonny got hit ... 27th Benny wounded, Johnny and Red badly wounded, Pete Beaton killed outright.'

Then – thankfully – there some relief, and also a delight: '4 Aug: climbed on top of pt.350 and had first look at Florence.' It had been a place of awe from my art courses at school.

Three days later we had three weeks' rest, and I visited Siena, which I found captivating: a lovely medieval city with its Piazza del Campo in the historic centre, where I learnt that the Palio di Siena was staged twice each year on 2 July and 16 August. As I looked at the now serene centre it was hard to envisage the 10 horses with jockeys riding bareback charging around on the thick layers of sand specially laid for each race, some jockeys often thrown off at sharp treacherous bends.

There was something surreal about such breaks – whether in Siena or majestic Florence or awesome Rome, with all their amazing history, art and culture.It was as if the carnage and blood of the war was on a different planet. But it certainly wasn't: it lay in waiting miles up the road we were due to drive along.

After Siena we 'lazed around and cleaned and serviced truck. Got pinched by the RP Sgt for firing shots from captured Mauser without permission. The RSM just warned us. Got two letters from Mom – a treat.'

A solider lying in a tent reading a letter from home

Infantryman in a tent reading a letter from home

Inside of a tent at Hay Paddock

Soldier in front
of a makeshift
tent - a bivvy

Goggles, at Hay Paddock

Above, sketch of Lt. Smith's patrol being opened up on from a Spandau machine gun-nest near Panzano on 22 July 1944. Our machine gunner Cellier is on the left next to platoon signaller with our wounded men on the right; below a sketch of one of our men, Hampson, taken prisoner by the Teds (Germans) on 21 July 1944 – he made a miraculous escape back to our own position

A direct hit on a
German Spandau nest

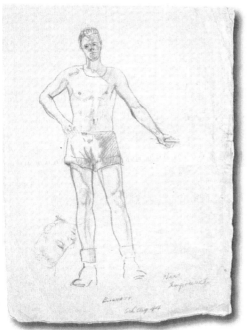

Loftus, near
Impruneta, 6 August,
1944

51

Infantry man with his
rifle over his shoulder
and carrying a shovel
for digging a slittie

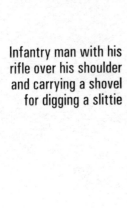

Loftus at Alassio

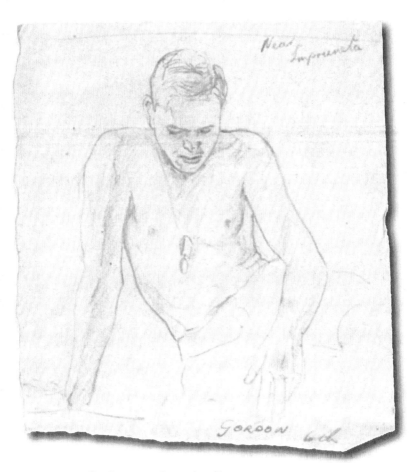

Gordon, one of our signallers, near Impruneta

Chapter 5

Pushing Onward

On leave in August I was thrilled to be allowed to travel back down the road with colleagues in an army truck to visit Rome. 'Went up to the Sistine Chapel and saw Michelangelo's wonderful frescoes on the ceiling. 'They seem to stand out in a 3 dimensional way, heaps better than the reproductions one sees … went to see the Colosseum and clambered all over it. It was very interesting and jolly impressive. In the afternoon saw 'A Canterbury Tale', excellent film. Went to see Aida at Opera that night but didn't enjoy it much as all dialogue was in Italian.'

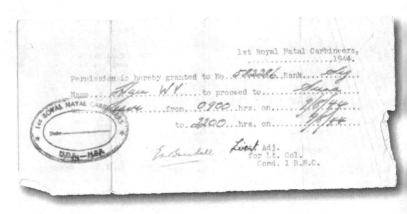

A Royal Natal Carbineers permission for me to leave my quarters on 9 August, 1944

Back on duty on 24 August, now chasing the nearby Germans again, we 'took over from the Yanks' and based ourselves at Podere Campolivo, a farmhouse near 'Caruso's Castle'. This was a palatial building once owned by the world-famous Italian tenor Enrico Caruso, and C Company's 10 Platoon was based there.

When a company was stationary for some time (as was C in this position), battalion HQ signallers would lay telephone cables along the ground to company HQ whose signallers did the same to their platoons,

54

with communication by telephone rather than radio. Thus at Campolivo my and Lanky's time was taken up with laying telephone lines to the platoons, then going out to repair the many breaks in these caused by what seemed like constant attacks from shells. There were casualties and deaths on both sides: 'We had to "keep our head and eyes moving" – as it's quite scary.'

My friend and fellow signaller Pete de Klerk used to say to me: 'I can always tell it's you coming back in the dark Wal, from your whistling.' I was known by family and friends to be a habitual whistler.

Above, Willy, one of signallers, posing for me;
below, Loftus posing for me

Fullerphone Operator,
Loftus at Podere Campolivo,
29 August, 1944

Drawings of Loftus at
Podere Campolivo

Above, the ox
house at
Campolivo,
August, 1944

Lanky at
Campolivo and of
a farm at
Castelguidi

57

Signalmen busy repairing
broken radio lines at
Campolivo

Dead German at Podere
Campolivo

Lanky, cleaning his nails at Campolivo (a very infrequent occurrence)

Just before going on patrol at last light, near Campolivo

On 25 August 'at about 0330 Staff Pike and Pop Castle (driver) came back (in ration jeep) from Caruso's Castle to tell us of movements heard. About 200 yards away Jerries jumped them, pulled Pike (Quarter Master Sergeant for battalion) out of jeep – apparently wanted prisoner – but he grabbed both their weapons and struggled. They shot him high up in thigh. Both he and Pop opened up with tommy guns, killed one Tedesco and rest miked off. Pop hit in legs and grazed under nose and along his back. Staff Pike hopped in jeep – too weak to put Pop in –managed to put it in low and came down to within 30 yards of Podere Compolivo – our house – then just before blacking out shouted "Maurice, Maurice" (our CO's driver) . Maurice shot out and collected him and everyone else ran to collect Pop. One of our guards put a bullet through the Jerry lying there (Loftus reckoned he was still alive. Dutch, our medical orderly, attended to Pike and Pop and jeep ambulance came up later to collect them). Went with Tubby and Rosie and 2 other linesmen to 10 platoon forward post (a listening post out ahead of their position in a house). All very eerie. Line eventually through around 12 o'clock. (mortar line from Tac direct to the post. I went to direct them to 10 platoon house). Everyone very tense because of last night's business. We heard today Pop Castle had died.'

The next day was also bad: 'Nicholls & Thompson of 10 platoon walked into AP mine and got chowed. Both bad, Nicholls in guts. Hear he is serious. Good chap.'

CHAPTER 6

Castiglione dei Pepoli

Moving on, we waded across the river Arno and on 2 September found 'good grapes and some lovely pears'.

Then, on the way up past the Tuscan town of Empoli over ten miles south of Florence, and on to Vinci, we took over a house 'where a girl in white raincoat was. She had many admirers but unfortunately she left.'

Next day, 8 September, we occupied another house. 'Went for a walk that evening. Country very hilly and looked beautiful in the afternoon sunlight.'

But sightseeing was secondary. Three days later: 'Tonight Mr Tirrel (8 platoon) collected 2 Jerries on sentry go. He and his patrol came up from behind them and took them without fuss. As they left they heard their guard commander calling to the two. Mr Edmunds' boys violently shelled, one killed his legs chowed, pulled back to our house.'

Well north of Pistoia, we had a lot of trouble laying a line to 8 platoon when a Spandau fired on the slope below us and above us. 'We got down quickly. The fellows in the jeep waiting to take us through Capo Strada and drop us at 9 platoon heard the reel going "clack–clack–clack" as it unwound laying the cable, then a burst of fire "rrr....rip", then "clack-ack-ack-ack" as Lanky accelerated. We did not linger.'

Amid the gruelling action, our lines were constantly shelled and needed incessant repairs and re-laying. But I was allowed a day off in Florence on 23 September. 'Saw the cathedral but didn't see any of the palazzos. Stood on the bank of the Arno near Ponte Vecchio, bridges on either side blown. Man in a skiff sculled gracefully along amid all the shambles.' The medieval Ponte Vecchio, originating from Roman times, was not destroyed by Germans during their retreat of 4 August 1944, unlike all other bridges in Florence, allegedly because of an express order by Hitler.

The next day 'Had a wonderful drive up hillsides with beautiful view down into deep valleys. The hills are thickly wooded with an occasional clear patch smiling up at you. Coming down you could hardly see the valley, the mist was over everything.'

Shortly afterwards we went into Florence for a break:'We got in after lunch and went to Apollo theatre to see Murder in Times Square and also Yank Engineer unit's show Bypass to Berlin – both were lukewarm. We came home in the moonlight and went right into Pistoia before the driver realised it.'

But, within a month, what seems looking back on it all the almost-charmed life I seemed to have lived amid all the death and injury swirling around me very nearly came to an end.

Before that however, on 2 October 1944 'moved up at about 5 in the morning through the small village of Castiglione dei Pepoli', a commune in Emilia-Romagna region twenty five miles south of the city of Bologna.

But I didn't notice the gentle glade on our left in which, forty years later, I would discover an immaculate South African cemetery had been erected to house so many of the army comrades now with me.

The farm cart, before Pistoia, 10 September, 1944

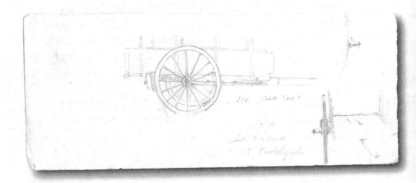

George, another of our signallers at Santomato, 27 September 1944

Portrait of Corporal Dutch, our Company medical orderly, above Carmignano 3 October 1944

A house our troops occupied in Carmignano, Italy 8 October, 1944

Trees and a leg in shorts

CHAPTER 7

Taking Stanco and on to Fateful Pezza

Although it was so quick and I had no time for self-contemplation, death nearly got me when we tried to take Monte Stanco, a hill which the Germans were holding.

On the way there, 'cleaning up' some Germans, we came upon a church standing proud on its own in a small hamlet, Vigo. It was a tiny rural church, and I 'got some big candles' which I fancied. But we also saw 'two SS officers, one very haughty though shot through the shoulder. The other shot through the cheeks with great gobs of blood and spit on his chest, moaning in a bewildered, animal-like way.'

It was cold with snow on the highest Apennine peaks as we moved towards the small Stanco mountain on 10 October, only too aware that a German SS infantry battalion was holding it. Amidst mud and rain, an Indian regiment had tried and failed to capture the stronghold, with fatalities.

Now it was our C Company's turn. One of their platoons was ahead on top of Stanco and chowed [killed] spans of SS who the Indians said came walking towards them saying 'Surrender Tommies. Hitler will treat you well'. We all thought they must have been drugged.

We went forward gingerly and parked up until our other platoons had gone into a casa at the foot of Stanco.

Mortars came over towards us all the time and fell quite close. As we came up the slope towards the casa through the vines, a Spandau opened up on Lanky and Loftus and I. Bullets zipped and snarled around us as we all threw ourselves flat and tried to go straight down into the earth. (Loftus had the 22 set strapped to his back, I had the 22 power pack and was carrying the battery and aerial tubes, Lanky had his 21 set strapped to his back). Lanky said he was hit then said 'No', and got up and jolled [jogged] for the casa and got there OK.

Then Loftus hopped up. They gave him a burst and a wine wire caught under the 22 radio on his back and whipped him to the ground. I thought he'd been chowed but they missed him. He hopped up again and ran for the casa. So I followed him, sprinting as best I could carrying the heavy pack. There was another brutal Spandau burst, shots screaming past like tracers in the air. I felt something slam right onto me, the sheer impact knocking me over, tumbling to the ground.

I was confused: had I been wounded or not? It was all too rapid to feel terrified, or even to understand. But I felt no burning or hurting sensation.

'I yelled to Lanky I'd been tonked and he came running back to help me but I found I was OK and told him just to show me a clear space through the wire. Then I got up and jolled, zigzagging along and they left me alone. I climbed through a window into a bedroom in the casa, a wounded German on the bed in a bad state and one of ours also wounded on the floor.'

Prisoners taken at Stanco before the Stanco stakes

Platoon Bren Gunner dug in to his slittie near Stanco 10 October 1944

Bren gunner

Post war painting of infantry men dug in near a farmer's barn

Sherman tank on a hilltop shelling distant German troops

Two Bren Gun Carriers

I was still bewildered about what exactly had happened. I didn't seem to be injured but still I had been knocked right over. Then – an explanation for my narrow escape: 'I found the Spandau bullet in my emergency bully beef tin in my Tommy pouch (over my heart), with the tip of the bullet bent'. Although its force had been so powerful as to flip me right over, the bullet had been blocked in the corned beef tin, miraculously saving my life.

But there was no time to dwell on my luck. No time to reflect or to worry, because our advance platoon had been 'shoved off Stanco', were instructed to pull out – and a German sniper was firing at the only door we could exit from.

'We called for a tonk on our casa then closed up shop. Cellier the Bren gunner fired some bursts and we went out one by one and gathered behind the casa, where we were hidden from the Germans on the hill. They took a shot at me as I rushed out and it went past my head. Then we all started to joll back and they were shooting at us. I could see little wavy blue smoke lines in the grass in front of me where the bullets were hitting.

69

It was really quite amusing (the whole mob careering across this field, discarding bits of equipment – Brens, Tommies, small packs etc – as they ran). Lanky took a mad tumble and I thought he'd been tonked but he'd only tripped and hopped up again. I was bloody tired with the 22 power pack, battery, aerials and telephones. We ran past a dead Indian, struggled up over the road till we got behind a rise then up over a little knoll. Then something burst about 1 yard ahead of me on the path. I just saw a flurry in the sand then a hole appeared. It blew the aerials out of my hand, missed Lanky ahead of me and a flat piece bounced off Loftus's neck cutting it a bit (probably a rifle grenade). We dug in for that night.'

Loftus in his slittie after the Stanco Stakes were completed on 10 October 1944, with his wireless equipment outside the slittie. The drawing done after the war was completed, waiting to go home, on 24 June 1945

Left, waiting to go out the door, then taking part in the Stanco Stakes on 10 October 1944. The drawing done after the war on 24 June 1945

Self-portrait of signallers watching German shells landing in Grizzana 15 October, 1944

Taking of Pezza on 17 October, the captured German portion, with their machine gun and the dead gunner; Below, on the slope up to Pezza, with slitties for signal officers and us on the 18 October; below, shows food containers which were delivered to us there

Italian country houses and a nearby fir tree, 20 October 1944

Three days later on 13 October two other South African regiments acting together finally pushed the enemy off Stanco and it was taken, despite a lone Spandau stubbornly still firing. The field we'd run over looked like a real battleground with equipment strewn everywhere.

A few days later, on the road to the village of Grizzana Morandi, 'I was 'molto paura' (very scared) by dozens of phosphorus shells and 17 October was a lousy day. Luckily had slitties dug for us. There were shells coming in like an express train. You'd hear them coming, reach their highest altitude then descend near us with a terrific rush and one killed Sgt Taffy – a good bloke. I was shit scared as you could hear the Spandaus going and mortars arriving – I was very pleased I was a radio operator and not an infantryman.'

'Eventually we arrived at where we were going and I tried to dig in – it was funny as I struck rock about 6 inches down. As we arrived there Pop Pretorius, himself slightly wounded, came shepherding along some Jerries. A couple were dressed in clean, creased uniforms and looked neat and freshly shaven. One had on that sort of kids-romper thing their paratroops wear, had both hands roughly bandaged, held them above his head and kept saying to the Boy Scout, "I am wounded in the hand Sir". He was a well-built bird. About 30 yds up were 8 pltn, with a dead Ted that Abe Braver had shot from the hip with his rifle. He had on spotted, tiger-camouflage pants. 9 Platoon were in pretty bad shape as Dennis Smith had been chowed by a Schmeisser at a couple of yards range – in the thigh. Also Taffy was gone and a couple of others were wounded.'

'This was about the lousiest possie I was in (Mt Pezza). My slittie was only about 6 inches deep and I couldn't go deeper on account of the rock. Shells used to land above us on our right, beside us on our right, and a regular every-day delivery of mortars below us where the mules came up. As always of course the platoons were worse off. Loftus and I went out that night across to B Coy [Company] simply by following the slitties which were about two yards away from each other in thick bush, then laid a line back. The imports which dropped above us on the right were big stuff – 170mm? – and were usually right on the line. One day they dropped a load and Lanky wanted to go out and fix it but I was too bang (scared) and said "hang on a bit". A few minutes later another lot arrived on the same spot. A bit later Lanky went out and shamed me into going too. The Boy Scouts' tin hat saved Lanky from getting his leg chowed here.'

Now came the fateful day on 21 October 1944 at point 806 on a damp, chilly Monte Pezza which could be seen high on the horizon from Monte Stanco . 'At 0400 hrs we moved past D Company and took over. The slitties were delightful. Loftus and Lanky were on the sets so I laid a line back. Then Lanky and I (who were sharing a wide slittie) started improving our one.'

We settled down to sleep. Suddenly 'at about 12 o'clock a piece of shell tonked me in the leg (having come through the access opening in the roof near our feet). The wound was in the right groin. I took my shell dressing and put it on my leg.' Lanky was screaming. 'I pulled him back into the slittie. Couldn't see any blood or anything on Lanky but he was moaning. Tried propping him up this way and that but all ways hurt. Then James and Dutch arrived and gave him morphia but made no difference.'

Brave, unarmed Indian stretcher-bearers rushed to the scene, lifting Lanky up and away. As I saw them accelerating amidst the chaos I hoped to hell he was ok.

There was piercing pain in my upper right leg, and I limped along trying to find my way to the medical centre set up in a house amidst trees, Casa Ruzzone.

On the way, 'Passed stretcher-bearers having a breather and they said Lanky was dead.'

The blunt, almost casual way they told me made it hard to absorb. Why Lanky? There, right next to me in the slittie? The deaths and injuries to comrades in action swirling around me over the last weeks seemed to have escalated. Shells and machine gun fire had brushed by me at Stanco. A bullet aiming at my heart had lodged millimetres away in my corned beef tin.

Looking back it seems uncanny for I suppose I always seemed to have been in just about the right place at the right time to miss injury or death – though I wasn't self-conscious about it at the time. I just pressed on, adapting to whatever was going on.

But this was of an entirely different magnitude. I had been wounded and, appallingly, my mate Lanky killed. Of course I knew back when I had first enlisted that war was dangerous. I had been scared a lot of the time. But I never really thought anything would happen to me – none of us ever did.

I was shivering, dazed and in a state of shock. At the medical centre I was given a new dressing and some hot tea. Then I was directed into an ambulance bound first for Grizzana. Our intelligence officer Stan Jones had been very badly wounded and was lying on a bunk in the same ambulance. I tried to talk to him but there was no response. He died right in front of me, before we reached the hospital, just seeming to drift away on the journey. After Lanky it was a second, dreadful shock.

Then I was transferred to a second ambulance to Castiglione and a third, the South African General Hospital at Florence. I 'tried to swass [urinate] in the ambulance but it hurt'. In Florence 'They put me into bed. Tried to swass again as I was full but hurt myself and yelled so a nurse came and gave me an injection.'

I was now desperately anxious: how badly was I injured? Would I be permanently disabled, would I survive?

'At about 0400 hrs on 22nd I went into theatre (operated on – they put a catheter through my belly into my bladder – the quack [doctor] called it my "super pubic" – with the other end into a bottle to relieve me).' After feeling I would burst, it was like being liberated.

Next day I was moved by ambulance, carrying my bottle with me, to the 31st British General hospital at Arezzo where they re-dressed me.

Then it was on by train to the 106 South African General Hospital in Rome. 'Ward Sister was young & knew a lot of the RNC [Royal National Carbineers] officers and blokes.'

Then came respite at last after being moved nearby and operated on at Rome's 48th British General Hospital: 'Went to theatre twice, bottle removed and started walking.' (The piece of shrapnel had entered in my groin and penetrated into the pelvis, missing everything important on the way. The surgeon decided it would do no harm leaving it where it was rather than trying to remove it).

Fifty-seven years later in London, I began feeling an uncomfortable lump protruding from the skin near my back passage. Although I had no idea what it could be, a surgeon discovered and removed the shrapnel: apparently it had travelled right down from my pelvis.

In Memory of
Private
G C Brasler

589232V, 1st Bn., Royal Natal Carbineers, S.A. Forces who died on 21 October 1944 Age 18

Son of Mr. and Mrs. A. B. M. Brasler, of Clanwilliam, Cape Province.

Remembered with Honour
Castiglione South African Cemetery

Commemorated in perpetuity by
the Commonwealth War Graves Commission

The commemorate plaque remembering Lanky Brasler.

Infantry being given a lift on a tank to the scene for action

Platoon Radio operator on his way into action

CHAPTER 8

The Final Stages

After being returned to the 106 South African hospital I was sent first across Rome to the Number 1 South African Convalescent Depot for 11 days – 'a sad place' – and then for a couple of days at 159 Transit Camp outside which I was able to enjoy evenings and afternoons in the city.

Infantry relaxing out of the front line in 1944

Then it was on the move again, by train to Arezzo and out to join the Reserves at Santa Barbara. 'A lousy joint. (Met John Aitchison and Gordon Boyack's brother here. Went on trip up through Castiglione by hitching to see Willie and Tom).'

By now I was deemed ready for action and assigned to the 13th Brigade Signals Squadron stationed 'in an eastern–mosque–type building about 10 miles outside Florence. Then to Santomato for a couple of days.'

Next I was allocated to the Natal Mounted Rifles (a tank regiment turned into infantry) at Bagnolo, about ten miles outside Florence, where it was great to meet up with my friends Loftus and Pete who visited me there. They wanted to know exactly what had happened to me, delighted I had recovered fully, seemingly with no after-effects. I also went to visit them at Lucca, and was also able to stay a night with my brothers Willie and Tom at Castiglione, before 'went on two manoeuvres'.

Now, however, severe winter months had halted the Allied advance towards the retreating Germans in the Apennines south of Bologna. I was billeted outside Florence in a large house owned by a wealthy family. It was snowing and I drew our tanks parked up and covered in white. With other troops, I was sleeping on the first floor and, to avoid the chore of finding a toilet, we all urinated out of the window, leaving little steaming holes in the snow lying on the ground: 'like piss holes in the snow' – decades later my children and grandchildren used to laugh at this, one of my many army sayings.

Afterwards the Allied advance began again and we 'Moved up to Gardaletta. Watched Thunderbolts bombing Mte Sole and also nice display of tracers by yanks at Mte Rimici. Was just across road from Pete and Loftus. Moved up at night towards Bologna. .... a lot of walking over the hills. Passed Yank infantry on the road next day were stocky, short chaps with alternate platoons armed with carbines and Garands. They had a Ted marching along with them who was even shorter than they were. Parked the night near huge anti-tank ditch.Arty [Artillery] near us lit fires and we were rewarded by being bombed – about 100 yds away.'

We moved on, delighted to see our planes bombing the enemy. Accelerating northward, destruction was everywhere. 'Every house along the road to Bologna had been attended to by Yank bombers and all the fields were pitted with craters – they simply saturated the whole countryside.'

'Teds had marvellous prepared positions in sides of hills – looked as though they could have hung on forever.'

North of Bologna, we parked up for the night: 'Either side of the road in beautiful fields in bright moonlight. Convoys were coming down the road with lights on, suddenly the rip of a Spandau burst. Lights out, screaming of tyres as brakes hastily applied. Had a couple of Jerry planes messing around all night. I was very jittery – heard a plane coming down towards us so got out of bed and sauntered towards a dyke, ostensibly to have a swass. Suddenly plane was on top of us, so I ran through pool and crouched against dyke wall. As the machine passed over me at about 50 feet it opened up with cannon firing over us at the road – I almost went into the dyke like a mole from fright. Tracers were drifting lazily up from

AA guns and some fellows were popping off with Tommies and Brens.'

We crossed the river Po and pushed on, with the German forces fleeing rather than fighting. 'After this it was all a great race. Went on through the flat country – never saw any hills – divided by small canals with trees planted along them.'

'Had a bit of a do in one village where Ites [Italians] and partisans were, as usual, dead scared of the Teds until our boys had taken prisoners, and then got very brave with them. There were about 10 Teds with guard surrounded by threatening yelling and cursing mob of Ites who sometimes had to be shoved back by guards. Our Scout car parked in street, pltns ahead and Ites all around, suddenly yells and everyone disappears into doorways leaving us alone in centre of street. Thought maybe a Tiger was coming round the corner and I'd get an 88 through my gizzard – was apprehensive in fact. Instead, one partisan with two Teds – one with black eye – materialised. Teds wanted to come with us but we pulled out and left them – suppose MPs [Military Police] took them from Ites.'

We then pushed towards Venice, and 'peasants lined roads, cheered and dished out eggs like good things.'

The deadening apprehension of conflict had now lifted, and in the days that followed there was time for a quick enjoyable look at Venice – another icon from my school studies – and later a trip round Lake Como.

On 'the night of 8 May 1945, Victory in Europe Day, there were celebratory tracers going up into the sky' and we left for Monza in a very slow, nose-to-tail convoy. I 'drove all night and at about 0300 fell asleep and hit a tree. Lt. McLaughlin almost passed out but I was quite amused by it all. If I hadn't hit the tree we would have gone over the edge into a huge ditch about 10ft deep which ran beside the road.' Fortunately nobody was hurt: 'the only damage was a bust spring'.

'Two LAD [Light Aid Division] chaps came along in their Volkswagen (captured) and while they assessed damage I took Rosso Smith for a ride in the little bus – it was fine and had quite a turn of speed. RNC scoutie passed us with much derisive hooting. NMR [National Mounted Rifles] LAD towed us to Monza where they fixed up spring and were very nice about it – no accident sheet. Then rejoined unit at power station. Taken to task by McLaughlin but laughed. Went two trips with him in his Jeep - drew lots for them both - one around Como and one up along Maggiore to Mte Rosa.'

Afterwards 'Monza Victory Parade – I wasn't on it – then to Torino. First with NMR across Po and then with Signals – and Pete and Loftus – Caserma Monte Grappa (military barracks in Turin).'

Italian Alpini hat from their 7 Infantry, sketched at Monte Grappa,10 June 1945

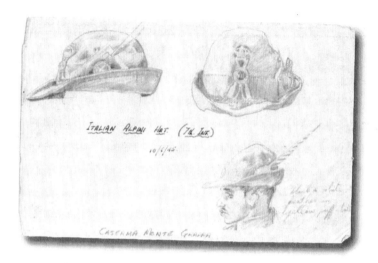

A country house at Parugiano

Sherman tanks and a jeep in the snow at 3 am
at a country house at Parugiano

Watercolour of the same scene at Parugiano

Ted Prisoner, Perugino

German prisoner waiting to be taken away from Parugiano

The war over, we waited to go home, frequently visiting the seaside resort of Rapallo, once for a week's leave in a rest hotel, the Albergo Grande Italia. 'Had wonderful 3-tonner rides down as the drivers used to give it big stick. The truck would be going flat out at about 60 when one of the blokes in the back would lean forward and shout through to the driver, 'what's the matter, is the petrol stuck?' The cry was always 'Faster!'

In Rapallo my friends persuaded me to try some alcohol for the first time; I had never touched the stuff, but it wasn't too bad when you got used to it. We also 'met fine mob of girls' from well-off families, one with a holiday home in the resort. My Italian improved rapidly and I was introduced to some of their parents, one an Englishwoman. When they called at her summer house in Rapallo I danced (for the very first time) with the girls and we all swam together in the warm Mediterranean Sea, having great fun in a platonic, innocent way.

For me this was something entirely fresh, for I had never had much contact with girls before. Their strict upper-middle-class parents would never normally have permitted their daughters to consort with Italian soldiers ranked as mere Privates. But when they discovered I had embarked upon an architectural degree and my friend Pete de Klerk was a teacher, our professional standing apparently made us 'suitable company' for their girls.

83

Assigned to guard duty for two weeks in Rapallo, I 'had good fun as the girls used to come and visit us at the door to Divisional HQ. (Once I gave Mara my rifle to hold for a few moments, to the consternation of everyone in sight!).' I had carried a rifle throughout the war, having been trained in the desert, but never fired a shot in anger.

I was also assigned to Serravalle car park for two weeks about 20 miles from Genoa on guard duty. 'Went there twice and on to Rapallo. Pete and the boys were at Rapallo then. Hitched lift in Yank weapons carrier (15 cwt open truck) which had a pile-up just outside Genoa – no one hurt.'

'Loftus, Pete, Viv Petersen, Baffi (Gordon), Phil and I shuttled between leave at Rapallo and Torino. As the truck came round the headland and good old Rap spread out before us we used always to chorus "home again." Torino and Rapallo were our home towns.'

'Were moved from Mte Grappa to Alassio, about 60 miles N of Genoa along coast near French border to get ready for returning home and spent some time there waiting to go home.

'Back for a week's leave at Rapallo. Div [Division] played Kiwis then (at rugby) and beat them.

'Heard we were leaving and hitched to Torino with Phil to say cheerio to Maria (back home at Moncalieri outside Turin from their holiday home in Rapallo), then down to Rapallo next day to do same (kissed the girls goodbye – the first time we'd kissed them!). Next week-end we were back again in Rapallo.

'Then left by truck to Novara, by train down Italy to Taranto.Crossed Med on "Medina Victory" – Yank ship – fine grub, fine conditions. Landed Port Said where Wogs (Egyptians) talked to us in Ite. Helwan for month (over Christmas and my 21st birthday) where met up with Pete and Viv again. Then to Cairo West and home by Dak (Dakota aircraft) stopping overnight at Kampala and landing at Waterkloof airfield north of Pretoria. Mom and Dad and Auntie Alice were there to meet me.'

Here my Diary ends. It was great being home again with my family – and safely home at that. But somehow there was a tinge of regret too. I suppose it was missing the intensity of the comradeship of what in retrospect for me had been a great and searing adventure. There was Italy, with its warm, friendly people, its incredible cultural and artistic heritage I had studied at school but never imagined experiencing.

Then of course there was the War itself. Writing this now it's obvious that the War so nearly cost me my life, just as many of my soldier comrades like Lanky Brasler lost theirs. Although I never really reflected on this at the time, it was also a War that must have been a profoundly formative experience for me as a young man. I have never been one to dwell on such things. I just got on with life, trying to do my best, but I suppose the War must have changed me, enlarging my perspective on life to one so much broader than that of a typical home-grown, young, white South African.

Nevertheless, James Bourhill's poignant assessment of our homecoming struck a real chord: 'The general public could not comprehend what their boys had gone through or how the war had changed them. The amusing anecdotes told by returned soldiers, the majority of whom had not seen the frontline, added to the misconceptions which censorship and propaganda had already inculcated into the national consciousness. In South African folklore, the Italian campaign is perceived as a great adventure, and the volunteers are justifiably proud to have taken part. But those few who experienced mindnumbing violence and fear, or comforted a friend in his final death agony, wanted nothing more than to forget.Life carried on and the images of Italy became hazy through the mists of time.'[2]

I never went back to Italy until 1985 when Peter arranged for me to retrace my route with his wife Pat and young boys, Sam and Jake, driving along our original route in his Volkswagen camper van, using my diary to guide us. My return was uncannily, in a way hauntingly yet also beautifully, different. My rusty old Italian came in handy when we arrived at Monte Stanco, now placidly gentle in the August sunshine, and a pensioner recounted his excitable, youthful memory of the firefighting and destruction he had witnessed.

In 1996, for the second time retracing the route, we spent quite a while scrambling around in hills and glades to find Point 806 where Lanky had died and I was wounded. We also searched around for the medical centre which had been set up in a house called Casa Ruzzone; it wasn't easy to be absolutely certain but I was pretty sure the large crumbling old farmhouse now surrounded by overgrown bush and trees

[2] James Bourhill, *Come back to Portofino: Through Italy with the 6th South African Armoured Division* (Johannesburg, 30 Degree South Publishers, 2011), p 493

must have been it: so utterly dissimilar, it was hard to recall and comprehend the world of war that had once been ours.

Afterwards we walked back down to where we had parked the car on the road our vehicles had traversed 50 years before. I stood by the roadside looking out eastward towards the A1 Florence–Bologna autostrada over foothills basking in the late afternoon sun. It was about the same time of day that I had left the Medical Centre and 'limped down towards the road, passing fresh troops coming through to take the next peak Pt 826, looking over hills and valleys reverberating to the crash of explosions and seeing the smoke rising from the shell bursts'.

Peter had videoed this return visit and, as I savoured the moment, he asked me on camera: 'Would you have done it again?'

My reply seemed obvious: 'When there is such a war, then you have to be involved. It's your duty. Yes, I wouldn't have missed it.'

Loftus on the Banjo at
Cuneo, 29 July 1945

Nobby Clarke, Cuneo, 29 July 1945

Halftrack at Cuneo 30 July 1945

Destroyed TED 75 Pak anti-tank gun

Above, Willy; below, Loftus

Farmhouse on Cuneo, Torino Road

Description of the farmhouse

Phil at Rapallo, waiting to go home 1945

yours at Rapallo

Yachts at Rapallo 1945

Phil on guard at Rapallo

91

Sketched after the war, a Bren Gunner taking prisoners back past a German tank disabled by the weapon lying on the road

Partigiani (Italian resistance against TEDs): top right, a TED; bottom centre one with blue or red neckerchief

TED light machine gunner,
Italian women farm
workers, TED anti-tank gun

Post-war sketches of
rifleman and a Tommy
Gunner

Cars and a man in a helmet

MT yams at Helwan, July '43

Perhaps the final word should go to Major General Evered Poole, General Officer Commanding of the 6th South African Armoured Division.

In an Address at our Victory Parade in Milan on 4 May 1945, he said: 'Let us carry on this great comradeship and esprit de corps that we have forged on the battlefields of Africa and Italy, through adversity and victory – that comradeship forged in the fire of War – and carry it with us into our country after demobilisation, so that we stand together in peace as we do in war – that we stand together against the cancer of racialism, and that we help build our nation on sound foundations, routing those attempts to imitate a rotten Reich, the type of which we have now annihilated.'

South Africa's tragedy was that his words were ignored and that it took nearly fifty years of struggle to end my homeland's own 'rotten Reich' – the tyranny of apartheid, ironically first institutionalised within three years of defeating Hitler's own racial tyranny.

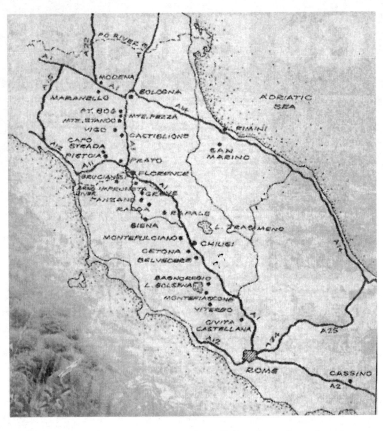

My own map of the route we took from Taranto northward

Official Commemorative Certificate of the 6 South African Armoured Division bracketed by the American Fifth Army and British Eighth Army emblems.

Signed by W H Everard Poole, General Officer Commanding

Shows from route from Taranto in the south to Milan, Turin and Venice in the north.

Appendices:

Example of Original Diary[3]

[3] The diary was intended for the year 1940, but I used it a few years later. The year and days in the original copy are therefore inaccurate

1 GIOVEDI   s. Pietro in Vincoli

on my leg. Couldn't see
any blood or anything on
hanky but it was moaning
Tried propping him up this
way & that but allways
hurt. Then James & Dutch
arrived & gave him
morphia but made no
diff. Heard Sgt Adams had
been killed, Stan Jones

2 VENERDI   s. Maria d. Angeli

badly wounded, Ray Kerslake
wounded also. Got my
small pack and a note from
Lt. Tipel to take to Maj.
Tomlinson who had taken over
C from Jelly when latter
wounded in foot by one of
our shells on Mt PEZZA.
Hist had casualties on.

Inv. di s. Stefano   SABATO 3

stretcher bearers had already
taken Stan. overtook Ray on
the way & he & I limped along
to B then up hill to Bn
& RAP. for leg was hurting
him a lot when he walked.
When I got to below R.A.P.
passed. stretcher bearers
having a breather & they

s. Domenico c.r.   DOMENICA 4

got new dressing at R.A.P.
then went down hill to
A.D.S. on way passing 1LH
going in to take B.26.
At A.D.S. had hot tea & watched
them give Stan a blood
transfusion. He was very
groggy & Col Comrie was
asking him who he'd

5 LUNEDI   B. V. della Neve

like to replace him & Ray
at C Coy. Then we climbed
into ambulance & they
shoved him in. Saw Edge
here too & he showed
concern. Went by amb.
round to Friggola where
saw Frykberg & were
transferred to 3-tonner

8 MARTEDI   Trasf. di N. Signore

Pommy ambulance wasn't
way down to Ripoli (?).
helped orderly give Stan
more blood. He was very
groggy & ambulance was
bucketing him. I told him
we'd soon be there.
came to C.C.S or something
at Ripoli (?) where

s. Gaetano Th.   MERCOLEDI 7

I've had more tea. They put
Stan on the table & made
me take off my boots & lie
down on stretcher & took
me into next room. After
a bit I asked an orderly
how the chap on the
stretcher table was & he
said he'd died but I

s. Emiliano conf.   GIOVEDI 8

was certain Stan couldn't
have died so asked again &
got no answer. was loaded
into another ambulance
& thence to Castiglione
where I was hoping
Willy & Tom would roll up
to see me. Told some
7/23rd sigs. to tell

ITALY DIARY 1944/45 - W.V. HAIN

These are verbatim from my diary except where in brackets, which are explanatory notes or additions. Willie and Tom are my brothers. 'Coy' means an Army Company, 'Ted' short for the Italian word for German – 'Tedesco'

Diary Entries before Rome

21st April 1944
Friday, landed at Taranto and came up to Gravina same day.

29th April 1944
Left Gravina and arrived at Boiano on 1st May.

3rd May 1944
Boys left and got into line at Cassino on night of 4th.

11th May 1944
At Fournelli at B Ech. Big push started.

15th May 1944
Johnson and I up to Cassino and into the line by N road.

22nd May 1944
Came out line to Fournelli. One day there then off to S. Agata near Naples. We had a mad march to just above Hove Dump, slept there and then marched to Aqua Fondata then caught the trucks home. Loftus and I were hungry.

29th May 1944
Left S. Agata for near Cassino.

31st May 1944
Arrived N of Pontecorvo. Latter is so battered is scarcely habitable.

Road sides here strewn with Teller anti-tank mines and box anti-personnel mines.

2nd June 1944
Left and passed Frosinone.

3rd June 1944
Parked next to Arty. Our boys giving it stick at Paliano. Carrier blown up; truck blown up next to us.

5th June 1944
Moving towards Rome to park otherside.

6th June 1944
In Rome. The natives are definitely friendly. Parked North of Rome.

Diary Entries after Rome

9th June 1944
Moved up about 5miles and got a 0.50 Browning and 20mm Solithern cannon for our carrier.

10th June 1944
Left early in morning and into Civita Castellana where we climbed all over the remains then on to North of Viterbo where we slept.

14th June 1944
Went on recce with carriers (might be here when on recce that an idiot in one of the other carriers fired his rifle, saying that he'd seen a Ted – short for Tedesco, Italian for German – but later admitted to us that he'd not seen anybody but had done it for a joke), After our recce B Coy went in towards Bagnoregio. Later parked near a sort of junk yard of abandoned German transport.

16th June 1944
Moving up, had fine ride along road on side of hill. See enemy demolition going up in distance. Slept with smell of something dead.

17th June 1944
Moved up to Belvedere and did recce. Had fine time, shelled a bit.

18th June 1944
Another recce also very nice. Slept below D Coy's objective where they had 7 killed. Dead Jerry aged 18 lying in trees. Two prisoners buried him. Grave too short so jumped on his ankles until these broke and then stuffed his feet in. His cross said "Died for Greater Germany".

21st June 1944
Has been raining in interim; moved up to Cetona. HQ in fine country house of a Count.

22nd June 1944
Watched M-10s (self-propelled guns) giving a house hell. Saw Loftus in a house on a hillside and got some magazines. Wonderful site but Huns have ruined pictures, furniture & library. Shelled a bit.

24th June 1944
Moved back to chicken house near Belvedere, then up to just outside Chiusi, where John R's lot got mucked up.

25th June 1944
Our blokes are in Chiusi. Watched Jerries shelling a road and saw Don R (dispatch rider) go for a loop.

26th June 1944
Moved into Chiusi. Roy and Mac wounded. Here now (1900 hrs). Got some good books. (Also the diary in which am writing).

27th June 1944
Out of Chiusi, messed around a bit and saw Basil. Moved about 3miles to where we'd parked on our messing about, near farmhouse.

28th / 29th June 1944
With A Coy HQ. Shelled a bit, A Coy had good show, killed 8 and took 11 prisoners, lost 2 killed.

29th June 1944

Moved forward with A Coy a bit, 5 prisoners just gone back – all very young (1926 lot). All wear Jerry fieldboots and grey trousers and long camouflage coat down to mid-thigh and Jerry caps.

30th June 1944

Up to little town with church. Stayed two days.

2nd July 1944

Out for rest at Montepulciano station, parked in house next to church, nuns gave us water. Our blokes buried dead Jerry and Ite priest read Last Sacrament over him. Everybody lit up (drinking) that night.

3rd July 1944

I transferred to C Coy, with Letsie and Gordon. Murgatroyd moved to carriers with Chris Londal. Heard Loftus and Phil Vile put up for Lance Jack (cpl). Loftus at Forward Control. 6th Field Artillery chap blown up by S mine linked to aerial bomb.

4th July 1944

Moved up and5th July 1944 moved again at 0530, are still on road, got shelled a bit. We are in drain ditch at roadside. One fell in the ditch about 40 yds away, but luckily round a bend. Saw Willie and Tom at their RHQ - Tom on set in scout car. Also saw Boet Tromp on the road. Pulled back to place we'd left that morning then moved up again at 2000 hrs and worked through the night.

6th July 1944

Nice lazy day.

7th July 1944

C Coy moved at about 2 in the morning and I went up about 1300 to Coy HQ on little road with Letsie. On 8th July 1944 in same place, shelled a bit.

9th July 1944 Sunday

Letsie copped it today. At about 1730 Letsie and I went to have a bath at the well at a little village, Rapale, about 400 yds away. The RDLI

103

were having grub so we hung around. Mr Edmunds (10 Platoon commander) was using the enamel bath. When he'd finished we filled it and Letsie washed. When he'd finished I took the bath round the corner to fill it at the well. As I was pumping the first shell landed - didn't hear the explosion so much as shrapnel whistling everywhere.I think it was this one that got Akker (Letsie – we called him Akker because he'd been circumcised so had an akkerpiel – acornprick). I dived next to the wall, RDLI blokes too. About 3 more arrived right on top of us. Masonry tumbled down just behind me. When all quiet I shot round the corner to find Letsie being attended to by a medical orderly – a shell had sliced off one leg above the shin and he was in a lot of pain. They had radioed for the MO and ambulance jeep. I went back to see what was going on and there were two men unconscious in the rubble. The RDLI blokes were there and it was decided not to move them – heard later they had died. I collected Letsie's clothes and took them to our possie near the road and when the ambulance jeep came past with him handed the clothes to them. Loftus came up to replace Lets in our team. So we are together again at last. Slept in the rain. Jerry shelled us at about 2 in the morning.

10 July 1944
Waiting to be relieved by 1st city. Moved out at about 2300 for new possie.

11th and 12th July 1944
At new possie (Palazzuolo). Slept all afty.

12th July 1944
Wrote letter today.

13th July 1944
0900hrs some twin engined bombers flew over. 1 shot down by Jerries. Moved into B Coy's possie. Gordon and I at rear. Loftus at CHQ.

14th July 1944
Got a letter from Mom, Dessie Buchanan wounded. Van and Dalton copped it yesterday afty on A Coy's line. D in neck, Van in shoulder. On guard tonight. Our guns pounded Jerry.

15th July 1944

Answered Mom's letter and slept all morning. Saturday today.

16th July 1944

Sunday. Chums (Brits) took over from us and we moved near Siena. Halted and had wonderful soak and washed. Saw most of the boys. We have another set in Maj. Mac's jeep now. Loftus operates. Moved again I was driving and was deadly. Heard Van had died and Issie Frank had been killed.

17th July 1944

Nothing much doing today. Boys moved out at app 1900 hrs. It is my turn to stay at rear and Gordon has gone with Loftus. Deadly. Tied into what I thought was our old line for Gil's phone. Turned out to be Bde line. We're still on it. On guard 1-2 in morning. Met Jack Brenner and friend on guard at their place and had an interesting chat concerning sappers (engineers) and their doings.

18th July 1944

We are about 3 mls short of Radda. Moved up after lunch. Sat on road til after nightfall then came into possie on hillside. Have just called Loftus on air & he has given me hourly scheds.

19th July 1944

Also there. Bakker (Lanky) and I picked up and re-laid line. Loftus and the boys returned. On guard 4-5. Arty gave it big stick.

20th July 1944

Moved on, Loftus in jeep, Gordon and I in the 15cwt (big pronto wagon). B Coy went in & took Panzano. Morrie standing 20 ft from Honey that had direct hit. Gerald Payne hit in Panzano near castle. Morrie in between him and Ite. Latter killed, Gerald seriously wounded. Morrie untouched. Loftus just around corner also unhurt. We walked from tpt passed Honey and on the way passed a burned arm lying next to it on the path. Walked just below P. and got into possie for night. Bit of shelling in early morning but Schubert's Serenade was playing on Lanky's 18 so everyone felt OK.

21st July 1944

Moved up to B Coy's platoon in white house & had brekker. The yard was a mass of jeeps and aerials. Sgt Barkley killed. Moved along top of ridge in jeep (Major, Sonny his driver, and Lanky, Loftus and I). Passed Sgt. Barkley's side pack & webbing – shell had burst about 5 feet from him. Passed Sherman which had bogie blown off by Teller mine. Went through to possie a couple of yards off road (my drawing of jeep at Panzano is here). Tanks above road. Bazooka & Spandau on corner. Expected shelling arrived a bit later. I was lying next to back wheel with earphones dangling next my head. Lanky above me and Loftus below. Shelling quite close. Spent chunk hit my boot about 6ins from Lanky's face, another ricochetted off left front wheel past my face into ground beside Lanky. German prisoner lying near us (not in slittie) didn't like shells at all. That night 9 platoon (C Coy platoons were 8, 9, 10) sent out patrol, challenged by Spandau crew. Mr Smith (platoon commander) shot 2 with tommy gun. 2 of our blokes missing. One wounded by sniper that afty. Doc (medical orderly) collected him. Boys killed 2 snipers.

22nd July 1944

Spasmodic shelling all day, Loftus hit very hard in arm by spent chunk (left dirty great bruise). One of fellows missing from last night's patrol turned up in his shirt and socks. Jerries had made him take off his boots and slacks, told him to take off his shirt. He saw a grenade on the ground, grabbed it, ducked round a bush, threw it back and ran. Dingo (small scout car) went up on mine we crossed over in jeep. In afternoon big war on. Mr Smith and patrol went to see about the spandau and ran full into it - Smith hit slightly, SM Corbett and McMorran badly. Bren gunner (Cellier) lying on ground got up and gave spandau stick. Jerry tommy gunned him and the bullets ran up the front of his helmet but failed to penetrate. Arty sent smoke, tanks went down and patrol pulled out OK. This show started ball rolling. Tanks below us firing madly at houses, M-10's (tank destroyers) behind us too, Vickers (heavy mg's) mortars etc. Now and then big Jerry shell would slam just below us. At last things died down. Wits & NMR went through. (Cellier was later awarded the MM. SM Corbett should not have been there at all as he was based at B Echelon, but he fancied himself as a marksman – had a rifle with telescopic sight and wanted to get a shot at the enemy! He recovered.)

106

23rd July 1944

Quiet day the odd shell came over. Next day (24th) transport came up and we moved to near B Coy. Had good night's rest.

25th July 1944

Moved up to new possie at 1645 hrs. Next day (26th) quiet – Sonny got hit.

27th July 1944

Moved up again today and Loftus and Gordon back at truck. Moved up at night and left Gordon with truck on road. CHQ on road on reverse slope of hill.

28th July 1944

Shelled. Benny Feinsinger wounded. Heard that Johnny (Johnson) and Red Lynham had been badly wounded back at A Coy transport, Pete Beaton killed outright.

29th July 1944

Parked there, found the apple orchard. Heard Gerald Payne had died. I went out with Arty O.P. officer (observation post) to operate his 18 set (and transmit his targeting instructions back to his guns) and watched Priests (self-propelled guns) shelling. Talked with Pete (now at TAC- tactical HQ – where the Colonel hangs out when the battalion is in action) on phone and he told me Johnny had died. (Note: Pete says Item 26 on Gerald incorrect. Pete had returned with Col from watching Florence being taken. Gerald took over from him in jeep. Jerry SP scored direct hit on jeep killing Gerald).

3rd August 1944

Moved up after dark to hill just south of Impruneta pt.350. Moon was out and beautiful walk. Came up off road and up past elegant slim white house. Passed TAC and spoke to Pete - he gave me 1st person Singular by Maugham. Got in very late.

4th August 1944

Climbed to top of pt.350 and had first look at Florence. Transport came up. Slept same place.

5th August 1944

Moved up in morning to new possie near D Coy - saw Pete and the TAC boys. Bakker (Lanky) tight tonight. 6th Sunday, the boys went to church service this morning. Gordon got 5 parcels.

7th August 1944

Left for new possie near Siena for 3 weeks rest. I drove half the way and was jumped on by Loftus and the others for my dead-loss driving. Left C Coy possie and came up to TAC. 8th lazed around.

9th August 1944

Loftus, Pete, Gordon and I went to Siena for the day. Looked over the cathedral and town hall. In the afternoon saw Will Fyffe at Ensa theatre. He was good. Met Boet Tromp coming out. He is transferring to the infantry. Hitch-hiked back to camp (just outside Castelnuovo).

10th to 13th August 1944

Lazed around and cleaned and serviced truckGot pinched by the RP Sgt for firing shots from captured Mauser without any permission. The RSM just warned us. Am reading The Light that Failed. Got 2 letters from Mom – a treat.

14th August 1944

Loftus, Pete and I borrowed a truck from Steve Morgan (the Captain in charge of our RNC signal contingent) and set off to find the 7th/ 23rd Artillery and eventually found them. Saw Willy and Tom. Both well but Tom is thin and needs some sun.

15th August 1944

Tom arrived in their scout car and Loftus and I went for drive with him to Rapolano.

16th August 1944

Going on leave tomorrow.

17th August 1944

Left for Rome at 0810. Had fine ride down, passed Lake Bolsena and also many knocked out Jerry tanks. In one place 2 Tigers, they look very clumsy. Got to rest camp at about 1430, had swim and on into Rome. Saw the Welcome Show at open air theatre. It was OK. Back to camp at about 2300.

18th August 1944
Into Rome, saw Pantheon and Vatican, both were super. St Peter's was marvellous and we could have spent the whole 3 days there. We went up to the Sistine Chapel and saw Michelangelo's wonderful frescoes on the ceiling. They seem to stand out in a very 3 dimensional way. They were heaps better that the reproduction one sees. We also saw the Pope passing by on his chair carried by 8 stalwarts. He was thin & jovial and blessed things held up to him as he passed. Saw some Brazilian troops in the audience. They range from "blonde Aryan" to "black savage". We trooped around a bit in the afternoon also bargained with prostitute in a bar – very funny - nothing came of it. Saw Buffalo Bill at the Ensa Supercinema. The NAAFI is a fine place. The Pantheon had a brown aura about it inside and was very impressive.

19th August 1944
Had our photo taken at NAAFIIn afternoon saw Yank play Over 21. It was very good. Went to ENSA concert in evening at Royal Opera House and saw one act of Madam Butterfly and Coppelia ballet. Latter was lovely. We have a fine drive alongside Tiber every morning. Rome is very clean, fine city with very good looking women.

20th August 1944
Went to see the Colosseum in morning and clambered all over it. It was very impressive and jolly interesting. In the afternoon saw "A Canterbury Tale", excellent film. Went to see Aida at Opera that night but didn't enjoy it much as all dialogue was in Ite.

21st August 1944
Came back to camp outside Castelnuovo

22nd August1944
Re-packed truck and went to Coys at about 1700. Barsdorf now with Loftus and I. Gordon at A Coy. Left at 1930hrs. through Siena, Poggibonsi and parked N of Castelfiorentino.

23rd / 24th August 1944
Parked all day and moved up in late afty and took over from Yanks
who left about 0200 on 24th. They seem very good chaps and have
good rations and lots of reading material. Had a lot of trouble with set
and phones but everything OK now - 1335 on 24th. I have collected
quite a decent drawing block at this house. HQ is at Podere
Compolivo house, platoons in other houses on farm.

25th August 1944
At about 0330 Staff Pike and Pop Castle (driver) came back (in ration
jeep) from Caruso's Castle to tell us of movements heard. About 200
yards away Jerries (4?) jumped them, pulled Pike (QMSgt for
battalion) out of jeep – apparently wanted prisoner – but he grabbed
both their weapons and struggled. They shot him high up in thigh.
Both he and Pop opened up with tommy guns, killed one Tedesco and
rest miked off. Pop hit in legs and grazed under nose and along his
back. Staff Pike hopped in jeep - too weak to put Pop in - managed to
put it in low and came down to within 30 yards of Podere Compolivo -
our house - then just before blacking out shouted "Maurice, Maurice"
(our CO's driver) . Maurice shot out and collected him and everyone
else ran to collect Pop. One of our guards put a bullet through the
Jerry lying there (Loftus reckoned he was still alive. Dutch, our
medical orderly, attended to Pike and Pop and jeep ambulance came up
later to collect them). Went with Tubby and Rosie and 2 other
linesmen to 10 platoon fwd post (a listening post out ahead of their
position in a house). All very eerie. Line eventually through around
12 o'clock. (mortar line from Tac direct to the post. I went to direct
them to 10 pltn house). Everyone very tense because of last night's
business. We heard today Pop Castle had died.

26th August 1944
Nicholls & Thompson of 10 pltn walked into AP mine and got chowed.
Both bad, Nicholls in guts. Hear he is serious. Good chap. In
morning Btn line found cut near dead Hun. No transport came up so
must have been cut. Capt Davis (our 2 I.C.) came back from Rome
leave with ration jeep.

27th August 1944
In morning Ites found another dead Tedesco about 30 yards below the

other. Ray ('I' corporal) and I went to Yank OP house and Ites there led us to him. So Pop & Jack got 2.

28th August 1944
Nothing eventful happened today. Tonight we had our 8 pltn line chowed to hell by a Sherman so Loftus, Lanky and I went out on it 9.30 pm. It was nice and moonlight so we felt OK. Found couple of breaks between 10 forward tee-in and 8 pltn then came to whole chunk ripped out, so went to 8 pltn to get reel of assault cable there, but Berkie had taken it, so we put in stray piece of Don 3, then caught a jeep back to Coy to find line still down, so we shot down there then shot back. We'd checked line but somehow missed a break. Got in at 0000 hrs. We keep our ears wide open and our "head and eyes moving" - as it is quite scary. I was second beat & spent my two and a half hrs reading Capt Davis' Readers Digest. Have finished "Honey on the Horn". It was fine.

29th August 1944
Did a sketch of grenades this morning – HE36, 69 Yank grenade & some rifle grenade thing. Also Loftus on Fullerphone. Had another session on the line tonight. First 9 got mortared and we fixed it up near Caruso's Castle. We'd just got back into bed when the tank at 8 pltn came up and did in 10 fwd and 8 lines. We fixed 10 fwd and were going down to 8 when we came on Pop Pretorius by himself with a rifle, fixing up a break. He says he knows Tedeschi (Germans) & they won't get him. Came back to 10 where Mr Edmunds told us the Mortar OP line was down. We fixed 2 breaks but it was still down.

30th August 1944
OP line went, Loftus and I went past 10 fwd tee in & fixed it. A mortar fell quite close. Came back and found 9 pltn line down. Tank had chowed it. We spent our time running in and out of the lodge each time a shell came into Caruso's Castle. We'd just found a break and were about to start fixing when we heard the first one coming and ran for lodge door - as we got to it a chunk hummed between us and considerably accelerated our progress. (More shells arrived onto C's Castle and we spent our time running and out of lodge each time one arrived). Came back here and went into dip on OP line, but no breaks. They once more shelled Castle from about 2230 hrs to about 0200 hrs

111

solid. 9 pltn had brush with Jerries and the Engineer officer who went out with Mr Edmunds has disappeared.

31st August 1944
9 pltn line went again in usual place. At about 1730 they dropped 17 shells on Castle, 7 direct hits. Liebenberg killed

1st September 1944
Moved across ARNO and past La Villa where we linked up with Loftus & the rest who had gone earlier and so on up to Artimino. Got in at last light and laid lines to the four platoons. Tubby and Cecil in linesmen's jeep followed us laying a line so as soon as we got there the line – to Btn - was through.

2nd September 1944
Good grapes here. After lunch, as at Campolivo, an Ack-Ack reg – Pommy - now acting as infantry took over and we came back. Loftus and I walked, Lanky was on the jeep and operated the 22. Loftus carried his mandolin he got in Artimino. I got an Ite children's reader very well illustrated. We waded across the Arno and stopped in Brucianese to wait for our jeep tpt to take us home. We had some lovely pears. This village is just below 10 fwd's old possie and it was this village that Zane went down to in civvy clothes (while the Teds were still there). We parked next to Tac - the old "Left Forward" exchange house.

3rd September 1944
Moved up after lunch through Empoli and on to Vinci where we are now. Barsdorf and I drove, Loftus travelled on jeep. Saw Sgt Jackson. 4th – 6th nothing much happened.

7th September 1944
Moved up to house where girl in white raincoat was. She had many admirers but unfortunately she left.

8th September 1944
Moved up again to old D Coy possie. On the way I hit a village – sarcastic comments from Loftus. Very nice house. Tac moved in just

112

after we got in. Went for a walk that evening. Country very hilly and looked beautiful in the afternoon sunlight.

9th / 10th September 1944
Moved up just short - about 6 miles - from Pistoia where I am writing this. 10th - good grapes here. I drew some farm carts today also Lanky in a cane chair, at Castel Guidi.

11th September 1944
Moved up to N of Pistoia in house on route 66. Laid line to Bill Wiles. Town is dead.

12th September 1944
Moved up to Ite hospital where most of the inmates seem to be loonies. That evening we moved up to house with fake columns above village of Capo Strada.

13th September 1944
Tonight Mr Tirrel (8 pltn) collected 2 Jerries on sentry go. He and his patrol came up from behind them and took them without fuss. As they left they heard their guard commander calling to the two. Mr Edmunds' boys violently shelled, one killed his legs chowed, pulled back to our house.

14th September 1944
No entry

15th September 1944
Laid line to 8 pltn and the tower Had a lot of trouble with line. That night Lanky and I laid to Outle's pltn. Laying back we reached the gates of 8 pltns houses when a Spandau fired on the slope below us and above us. We got down quickly. The fellows in the jeep waiting to take us through Capo Strada and drop us at 9 pltn heard the reel going "clack–clack–clack" as it unwound laying the cable, then a burst of fire "rrr....rip", then "clack-ack-ack-ack" as Lanky accelerated. We did not linger.

16th September 1944
Lanky and Loftus got to 8 pltn, heard a noise, looked around and saw some mortars land on our line. They didn't feel too happy and found one had landed on the line. That night the CHQ guard fired two bursts from tommy gun at the 10 pltn post but luckily missed him.

17th September 1944
George came up tonight. Line went down at about 2300hrs on the 17th by shellfire.

18th September 1944
So Lanky and I went out at about 0700 hrs. There were about 7 breaks, with big shell holes right next to the line. I sprained my ankle jumping a ditch. Tonight FC/CTH took over and we pulled back through Pistoia to where our tpt was.

19th September 1944
Moved up to where we are now at

20th / 21st /22nd September 1944
Loftus now full cpl went to Tac and saw Pete. Played soccer.

23rd September 1944
Went into Florence for the day. Saw Over 21 again & enjoyed it more than ever. Saw the cathedral but didn't see any of the palazzos. Stood on bank of Arno near Ponte Vecchio, bridges on either side blown. Man in skiff sculled gracefully along amid all the shambles.

24th September 1944
Left at 0700 for new possie. Very misty. Took over from our armoured inf friends (NMR?). Had a wonderful drive up hillsides with beautiful view down into deep valleys. The hills are thickly wooded with an occasional clear patch smiling up at you. Coming down you could hardly see the valley, the mist was over everything. A, B and D Coys parked near us. I am back at transport this trip.

25th September 1944
Nothing

26th September 1944
Loftus visited me to-day. Men came back to transport tonight and we
moved to new possie at Santomato.

27th September 1944
Drew George (Barsdorf) eating grapes and also tonight did portrait of
him by light of inspection lamp.

28th September 1944
Loftus hurt his knee

29th September 1944
nothing

30th September 1944
Went to Florence today with Loftus and George. Mr Smith drove and
we passed everything on the road. We got in after lunch and went to
Apollo theatre to see Murder in Times Square and also Yank Engineer
unit's show Bypass to Berlin - both were lukewarm. We came home in
the moonlight and went right into Pistoia before the driver realised it.

1st October 1944
Went to see Peter at Support Coy, visited two houses and talked.
Moved up through Bagnolo and Prato up to Montepuiano and parked
there that night right behind 5 5s (artillery).

2nd October 1944
Moved up at about 5 in morning through Castiglione up to Camugnano
and took over from 1LH. Rained a lot but no shelling. Charras
(Indians) took over from us and we moved on at and stayed in house.

3rd October 1944
Moved forward in morning and went on to Vigo church, waiting en
route while A and B cleaned up some Teds on the hill. Saw two SS
offrs, one very haughty though shot through shoulder. The other shot
through cheeks with great gobs of blood and spit on his chest, moaning
in a bewildered animal-like way.Got some big candles at church. Arty
had chowed it just before we got there. Moved on to another little

115

village. Here we met Chiesa family – father mother & Maria. Stayed there some then heard Charras had been chowed on Stanco.

9th October 1944
Moved on into Collina. Stayed there that night.

10th October 1944
Moved up to Stanco. B and D went in on to Stanco, then the SS came in behind D on the right. Could hear John (Popadopolous – Greekie) calling for D.F.s (Defensive Fire) very urgently on 22, also saying Teds coming in on right. D got thrown off – had no ammo left, – chowed spans of SS who they said came walking towards them saying "Surrender Tommies Hitler will treat you well". (D thought they were drugged). We went up and parked with A until platoons had gone into some casas (at the foot of Stanco), then the Boy Scout (C Coy commander) took Coy HQ to them. They must have been watching us all the time from Stanco.

Mortars came over all the time on the way and fell quite close. As we came up towards the casa through the vines a Spandau opened up on Lanky & Loftus & I. We all fell flat and tried to go straight down into the earth (Loftus had the 22 set strapped to his back, I had the 22 power pack and was carrying the battery and aerial tubes, Lanky had his 21 set strapped to his back). Lanky said he was hit then said No, and got up and jolled for the house & got there O.K. Then Loftus hopped up. They gave him a burst and a wire of the vine caught the 22 on his back and whipped him to the ground. I thought he'd been chowed but they missed him. He hopped up again and ran for the casa. I got up and hammed and they gave me a burst - I felt something slam me and the other shots from the burst seemed to press past me. I yelled to Lanky I'd been tonked and he left his 18 in the casa and came running back to collect me but I found I was O.K. and told him just to show me a clear space through the wire then I got up and jolled, zig-zagging along and they left me alone. (I climbed through a window into a bedroom). There was a wounded Ted on the bed looking in a sad state and one of our peas on the floor, also wounded. We slammed the 22 together and Loftus got through O.K. I found the Spandau bullet in my emergency bully tin in my Tommy pouch (over my heart, with the tip of the bullet bent. The bedroom floor was covered in apples from

the Ites' harvest). B got shoved off Stanco so we were told on the air
to pull out too. (I think that an ambulance jeep came up and took out
the two wounded before we left). Some Ted was firing at the only door
we could get out of. We called for a stonk on our casa then closed up
shop and went out the door. (Before we left Cellier the Bren gunner
fired some bursts up in his general direction. We went out one by one
and gathered behind the casa, where we were hidden from the Teds on
the hill). They took a shot at me as I shot out and it went past my head.
9 & 10 pluns were with us. Then we all started to joll back and they
were shooting at us like a good thing. I could see little wavy blue
smoke lines in the grass in front of me where the bullets were hitting.
It was really quite amusing (the whole mob careering across this field,
discarding bits of equipment – Brens, Tommies, small packs, etc. – as
they ran). I saw Lanky take a mad tumble and thought he'd been
tonked but he'd only tripped and hopped up again. I was bloody tired
with the 22 power pack satchels and telephones. (There was an
opening in the fence at the end of the field onto a road and we all
funnelled through it, with Stan Jones shouting "don't bunch, don't
bunch". We ran past a dead Indian in the road). We struggled up over
the road till we got behind a rise then up over a little gnoll. Then
something burst about 1 yard ahead of me on the path. I just saw a
flurry in the sand then a hole appeared. It blew the aerials out of my
hand, missed Lanky ahead of me, and a flat piece bounced off Loftus'
neck cutting it a bit (probably a rifle grenade). We dug in behind A
fwd section for that night.

11th October 1944
Moved over hill behind us and dug in on reverse slope (i.e. on side
opposite enemy). Was very steep and if anyone in top slitties where
we were - dislodged anything the peas below used to collect it –
particularly Gilly Cowan. Wits Tac was just below us in a house where
we washed and got apples. (12th in same possie – saw jeep driver on
road below put a wheel over the edge and the jeep roll over and onto
him. Also saw early morning Jerry recce plane leaving contrails).

13th October 1944 (Friday)
Wits & 1st City took Stanco today. Had quite a few chowed. Long
after they were supposed to have taken Stanco there was a Spandau
firing from behind them.

14th October 1944

Our peas went to collect the Brens & Tommy's they'd dropped in the gallop. Lanky and I went along too. The place looked like real battleground with equipment strewn everywhere. I think they had not yet removed the Charra who must have been there over a week but was not yet humming.

When we came past early on morning of 15th or 16th he was gone. (Ites had removed his boots).

15th or 16th October 1944

We got along road to Grizzana quite safely. I was molto paura (very scared) as I'd sat the day before and watched them throw dozens of phosphorus shells on the road & in Grizzana. Nothing happened tho and we got on to the hill above Grizzana with pylons on quite O.K., plus 2 brand new Jerry phones (much better than ours). Our Coy HQ. together with Morry's (B Coy) so had about 10 peas to do the shift. (Supplies came up by mules). Mules were always chowing our platoon line but left Morry's alone.

16th or 17th October 1944

Our line went at about 0100 hrs after some shelling. Loftus and I found the break and fixed it very quickly. Moved forward again and travelled with B Coy HQ. Loftus & I. A lousy day. Went up past D Coy. Luckily Maj. Gallymore (B Coy comm) has had slitties dug for us, as there was some stuff arriving. While we parked in the slitties there were shells coming in just like an express train. You'd hear them coming, reach their highest altitude then descend near us with a terrific rush. They were landing next to 9 Pltn and killed their Sgt. Taffy – a good pea. First Morry & Maj Gally moved, then we moved back then forward along track. I was shit-scared as you could hear Spandaus going and mortars arriving (we could hear the pltn commander shouting to his men "get that Spandau" – I was very pleased that I was a radio operator and not an infantryman). Eventually we arrived at where we were going and I tried to dig in – it was funny as I struck rock about 6" down. As we arrived there Pop Pretorius, himself slightly wounded, came shepherding along some Jerries. A couple were dressed in clean, creased uniforms and looked neat and freshly shaven. One had on that sort of kids-romper thing their paratroops wear, had both hands roughly bandaged, held them above his head and kept saying to the Boy Scout, "I am wounded in the hand Sir". He was a well-built bird. About 30 yds up were 8 pltn, with a dead Ted that Abe Braver had shot from the hip with his rifle. He had on spotted, tiger-camouflage pants. 9 Pltn were in pretty bad shape as Dennis Smith had been chowed by a Schmeisser at a couple of yards range – in the thigh. Also Taffy was gone and a couple of others were wounded.

This was about the lousiest possie I was in (Mt Pezza). My slitty was only about 6" deep and I couldn't go deeper on account of the rock. Shells used to land above us on our right, beside us on our right, and a regular every-day delivery of mortars below us where the mules came up. As always of course the pltns were worse off. Loftus and I went out that night across to B Coy simply by following the slitties which were about two yards away from each other in thick bush, then laid a line back. The imports which dropped above us on the right were big stuff – 170mm? – and were usually right on the line. One day they dropped a load and Lanky wanted to go out and fix it but I was too bang (scared) and said "hang on a bit". A few minutes later another lot arrived on the same spot. A bit later Lanky went out and shamed me into going too. The Boy Scouts' tin hat saved Lanky from getting his leg chowed here.

18th or 19th October 1944
The Wits came through us bound for 826, but they were chowed and got to 806.

20th October 1944
At night we moved over the hill and along past D and the RAP (Regimental Aid Post) and down to where B was. The Wits Coy Cmdr wouldn't' move out that night so we slept on the hill above B. It was very cold and there were some unpleasant bangs in the night.

21st October 1944
At 0400 hrs we moved past B and took over. The slitties were delightful. Loftus and Lanky were on the sets so I laid a line back to Morry. Then Lanky and I (who were sharing a wide slitty) started

improving our slitty. We dug deeper and wider and put up a roof (of branches with soil on top) and felt safe as a house. At about 10 o'clock the shells came on hill above to our left and below us but we felt very safe and were trying to sleep.

Then at about 12 o'clock a piece tonked me in the leg (having come through the access opening in the roof near our feet. The wound was in the right groin and I quickly put my hand down to make sure the family jewels were intact – they were). Lanky shouted "I've been hit, I've been hit" and I said "so have I". He jumped up onto the side of the slitty, another one arrived and he grabbed his back and screamed "Oh mama, mama, mama," and I pulled him back into the slitty. He lay back but was having a bad time. I took my shell – dressing and put it on my leg. Couldn't see any blood or anything on Lanky but he was moaning. Tried propping him up this way and that but all ways hurt. Then James and Dutch arrived and gave him morphia but made no difference. (He was sure he wasn't going to make it and asked me to go and see his sister, but I told him he'd be alright and the stretcher bearers would soon be coming). Got my small pack and note with list of casualties from Lt. Tirrel to take to Maj. Tomlinson who had taken over B from Gally when latter wounded in foot by one of our own shells on Mt Pezza. Heard Sgt Adams killed, Stan Jones badly wounded, Ray Kerslake wounded.Stretcher bearers had already taken Stan. Overtook Ray on the way and he and I limped along to B then uphill to D and RAP at Casa Ruzzone. His leg was hurting him a lot when he walked. When I got to below RAP passed stretcher bearers having a breather and they said Lanky was dead.

Got new dressing at RAP then went down hill to ADS (Advanced Dressing Station), on the way passing ILH going in to take 826. At ADS had hot tea and watched them give Stan a blood transfusion. He was very groggy and Col Comrie (Battalion CO) was asking him who he'd like to replace him and Ray at C Coy. Then I climbed into ambulance and they shoved Stan in. Saw Edge (a signals officer) and he showed concern. Went by ambulance round to Grizzana where saw Frykberg (another signals officer) and we were transferred to 3-tonner Pommy ambulance. On way down to Ripoli helped orderly give Stan more blood. He was very groggy and ambulance was hurting him. I told him we'd soon be there. Came to CCS (casualty clearing station) or something at Ripoli? where I had more tea. They put Stan on the table and made me take my boots off and lie on a stretcher then took me into next room. After a bit I asked an orderly how the chap on the table was and he said he'd died but I was certain Stan couldn't have died so asked again but got no answer. Was loaded into another ambulance and taken to Castiglione where I was hoping Willie and Tom would roll up to see me. Told some 7/23rd signals (Willie and Tom's lot) who looked into the ambulance to tell Willie and Tom I'd been hit but was O.K., but the message wasn't passed on. Then into nog 'n ambulans (another ambulance) and down to Firenze to 108 (SA General Hospital at Florence). Tried to swass in the ambulance but couldn't and it hurt when I tried. At 108 they put me into bed. Tried to swass again as I was full but hurt myself and yelled so nurse came and gave me an injection. At about 0400 hrs on 22nd I went into theatre & so on (operated on – they put a catheter through my belly into my bladder – the quack called it my "super-pubic" – with the other end into a bottle to relieve me).

23rd October 1944
Moved by ambulance to 31st British General at Arezzo, carrying my bottle with me. They re-dressed me here.

? October 1944
By train to 106 SA General in Rome. Ward Sister was young & knew a lot of the RNC officers and blokes.

? October 1944
Moved to 48th British General. Went to theatre twice, bottle removed and started walking (The piece of shrapnel had entered in my groin and penetrated into the pelvis, missing everything important on the way. The surgeon decided it would do no harm leaving it where it was rather than trying to remove it).

? October 1944
Back to 106.

? October 1944
To No 1 SA Convalescent Depot in Rome for 11 days – sad place.

A couple of days at 159 Transit Camp outside Rome - had two afternoons and evenings in the City. The camp was next to the aqueduct of?

By train to Arezzo and out to the Reserves at Santa Barbara. A lousy joint. (Met John Aitchison and Gordon Boyack's brother here. Went on trip up through Castiglione by hitching to see Willie and Tom).

To 13th Brigade Signals Squadron in an eastern–mosque–type building about 10miles outside Florence. Then to Santomato for a couple of days.

Assigned to NMR (Natal Mounted Rifles, a tank regiment turned into infantry) at Bagnolo. Bunny Tromp (Boet's brother) is a platoon commander here. Pete paid me a visit here then Loftus did. Went to visit them at Lucca. Stayed night with Willie and Tom and came back next morning. Went on two manoeuvres.

Moved up to Gardaletta. Watched Thunderbolts bombing Mte Sole and also nice display of tracers by yanks at Mte Rimici. Was just across road from Pete and Loftus.

Moved up at night towards Bologna. Coys did a lot of walking over the hills. Passed Yank infantry on the road next day – were stocky, short chaps with alternate pltns armed with carbines and Garands. They had a Ted marching along with them who was even shorter than they were. Parked the night near huge anti-tank ditch.Arty near us lit fires and we were rewarded by being bombed – about 100 yds away.

Next day moved up through Casa Lecchio which was a shamblesEvery house along the road to Bologna had been attended to by Yank bombers and all the fields were pitted with craters - they simple saturated whole countryside. Teds had marvellous prepared positions in sides of hills – looked as though they could have hung on forever. Parked the night on long straight north of BolognaTransport on either side of road in beautiful fields in bright moonlight. Convoys were coming down road with lights on, suddenly the rip of a Spandau burst, lights out, screaming of tyres as brakes hastily applied. Had a couple of Jerry planes messing around all night. I was very jittery – heard a plane coming down towards us so got out of bed and sauntered towards a dyke, ostensibly to have a swass. Suddenly plane was on top of us so I ran through pool and crouched against dyke wall. As the machine passed over me at about 50 feet it opened up with cannon and mg's firing over us at the road – I almost went into the dyke like a mole from fright. Tracers were drifting lazily up from AA guns and some fellows were popping off with tommies and Brens. Crossed Po.

After this it was all a great race. Went on through the flat country – never saw any hills – divided by small canals with trees planted along them.

Had a bit of a do in one village where Ites and partisans were, as usual, dead scared of the Teds until our boys had taken prisoners, and then got very brave with them. There were about 10 Teds with guard surrounded by threatening yelling and cursing mob of Ites who sometimes had to be shoved back by guards. Our Scout car parked in street, pltns ahead and Ites all around, suddenly yells and everyone disappears into doorways leaving us alone in centre of street. Thought maybe a Tiger was coming round the corner and I'd get an 88 through my gizzard – was apprehensive in fact. Instead, one partisan with two Teds – one with black eye – materialised

Teds wanted to come with us but we pulled out and left them – suppose MP's took them from Ites. After that up towards Venezia. Peasants lined roads, cheered, and dished out eggs like good thing. Into Venezia for an afternoon in my truck.

Left that night for Monza at 7.30. (Very slow nose-to-tail convoy). Drove all night and at about 0300 fell asleep and hit a tree. Lt. McLaughlin almost passed out but I was quite amused by it all. Only damage was bust spring. If I hadn't hit the tree we would have gone over the edge into a huge ditch about 10ft deep which ran beside the road. Two LAD chaps came along in their Volkswagen (captured) and while they assessed damage I took Rosso Smith for a ride in the little bus – it was fine and had quite a turn of speed. RNC scoutie passed us with much derisive hooting. (This was the night of 4 May 1945, Victory in Europe Day and there were celebratory tracers going up into the sky during our trip).

NMR LAD. towed us to Monza where they fixed up spring and were very nice about it – no accident sheet. Then rejoined unit at power stationTaken to task by McLaughlin but laughed. Went two trips with him in his Jeep - drew lots for them both - one around Como and one up along Maggiore to Mte Rosa. Monza Victory Parade – I wasn't on it - then to Torino. First with NMR across Po and then with Signals - and Pete and Loftus - in Caserma Monte Grappa (military barracks in Turin).

Then while waiting to go home began going down to Rapallo (where we had rest hotel – Albergo Grande Italia) from Torino for week's leave. Had wonderful 3-tonner rides down as the drivers used to give it big stick. The truck would be going flat out at about 60 when one of the peas in the back would lean forward and shout through to the driver "what's the matter, is the petrol stuck?" The cry was always "Faster"!

Spent 2 weeks at Cuneo with Loftus working link for D.S.R. lousy mob, lousy job.

Came back to Monte Grappa and worked on 299 (wireless set) to Div at Maggiore – was quite a set. When you bashed the key (transmission was in Morse Code) all you could see all over the place were meters with their pointers waving.

Some more of Rapallo. Met fine mob of girls there.

Then to Serravalle car park for two weeks about 20 miles from Genoa (on guard duty). Went there twice and on to Rapallo. Pete and the boys were at Rapallo then. Hitched lift in Yank weapons carrier (15 cwt open truck) which had a pile-up just outside Genoa – no one hurt.

Loftus, Pete, Viv Petersen, Baffi (Gordon), Phil and I shuttled between leave at Rapallo and Torino. As the truck came round the headland and good old Rap spread out before us we used always to chorus "home again." Torino and Rapallo were our home towns.

Were moved from Mte Grappa to Alassio, about 60 miles N of Genoa along coast near French border to get ready for returning home and spent some time there waiting to go home.

Had two weeks Div guard at Rapallo - good fun as the girls used to come and visit us at the door to Div HQ. (Once I gave Mara my rifle to hold for a few moments, to the consternation of everyone in sight!).

Back for a week's leave there. Div played Kiwis then (at rugby) and beat them.

Heard we were leaving and hitched to Torino with Phil to say cheerio to Maria (back home at Moncalieri outside Turin from their holiday home in Rapallo), then down to Rapallo next day to do same (kissed the girls goodbye – the first time we'd kissed them!). Next week-end we were back again in Rapallo.

Then left by truck to Novara, by train down Italy to Taranto.

Crossed Med on "Medina Victory" – Yank ship – fine grub, fine conditions. Landed Port Said where Wogs (Egyptians) talked to us in Ite.

Helwan for month (over Christmas and my 21st birthday) where met up with Pete and Viv again.

Then to Cairo West and home by Dak (Dakota aircraft) stopping overnight at Kampala and landing at Waterkloof airfield north of Pretoria. Mom and Dad and Auntie Alice were there to meet me.

Biographical Notes

Walter Hain

Born 29 December 1924 in Northdene, Durban, South Africa Walter Hain went to Arcadia Primary schools in Pretoria, and both Parktown High School, Johannesburg, and Pretoria Boys High School. He gained his degree in architecture at the University of Witwatersrand, later specialising in the design of hospital laboratories. At school he played cricket (continuing until aged 80) and rugby. He also follows golf and football as a keen Chelsea FC fan.

On 1 September 1948 Walter married Adelaine Stocks who was born in Port Alfred, South Africa, and they had four children: Peter, Tom, Joanne and Sally. The couple lived first in Pretoria, then briefly in Nairobi, Kenya; Port Elizabeth, Pietermaritzburg, Ladysmith, Pretoria, Ealing in London; Ruckinge, Kent and again Pretoria. By 2015 they had eleven grandchildren and seventeen great grandchildren.

Both Walter and Adelaine joined the South African Liberal Party in 1954 and from 1958 became extremely active in its Pretoria Branch, he its Chairman, she its Secretary until they were banned. For their anti-apartheid activism in the Party, the couple with both imprisoned for two weeks without charge in 1961 and then successively issued with banning orders, she in 1963 and he in 1964, designed to suppress their activism. As the first such married couple to be banned, an embarrassed Government was forced to insert new and special clauses in their Banning Orders enabling them to talk to each other, exceptionally as banned persons who were normally prevented from communicating.

Eventually in March 1966 they were forced to leave their beloved South Africa because they were deprived of earning an income after the Government instructed all architectural firms in Pretoria municipality – to which he was restricted by his banning order – from employing him.

The family moved to Britain where they lived in Putney for several decades. In 2009 Walter and Adelaine moved to Neath, South Wales.

For their story see *Peter Hain, Ad & Wal: values, duty, sacrifice in Apartheid South Africa* (Biteback, 2014).

Walter is the author of a widely used architectural design guide, *Laboratories* (E & FN Spon, 1995), and over his active life regularly wrote political articles and letters for national newspapers and magazines.

Peter Hain

Born in 1950 and brought up in South Africa, he has been in politics for over 50 years. He was Labour MP for Neath 1991-2015 and served in the governments of Tony Blair and Gordon Brown for twelve years, seven in the Cabinet. In October 2015 he became Lord Hain of Neath.

Peter was British anti-apartheid leader, especially in stopping all-white South African sports tours from 1969 onwards and is the author of 20 books. His memoirs *Outside In* were published by Biteback in 2012 and his biography, *Mandela* by Spruce in 2010. His ministerial diaries, *The Hain Diaries 1997-2008* were published by Biteback as an eBook in 2015.

Matthew Ward

He graduated in History and Politics at the University of York in 2014 before taking a Master of Philosophy in History from the University of Cambridge; he has also worked as a Parliamentary Researcher for Labour MPs Peter Hain and Madeleine Moon.

The Castigleoni Cemetery in the snow. In the cemetery there is a
memorial building originally erected by South African troops, which
contains two tablets unveiled by Field-Marshal Smuts; they bear the
inscription in English and Afrikaans:

TO SAVE MANKIND YOURSELVES YOU SCORNED TO SAVE
OM DIE MENSDOM TE DIEN HET JUL VEILIGHEID VERSMAAD